Letters to Georgian Friends

Как изваянья — бонн и кормилиц
И кустов на речном берегу,
Море грохнет, воздев на дыбы
Целый мир, целый город в снегу.

28
Вакханалия.

Город. Зимнее небо.
Тьма. Пролеты ворот.
У Бориса и Глеба
Свет, и служба идет.

Лбы молящихся, ризы
И старух шушуны
Свечек пламенем снизу
Слабо озарены.

А на улице вьюга
Все смешала в одно,
И пробиться друг к другу
Никому не дано.

В завыванье бурана
Потонули, мертвы,
Электрички, экраны,
Новостройки, дома.

Клочья репертуара
На афишном столбе
И деревья бульвара
В серебристой резьбе.

Part of a letter to S. I. Chikovani showing the poem
Vachkanalija (Bacchanalia)

Boris Pasternak

Letters to
Georgian Friends

TRANSLATED FROM THE RUSSIAN
WITH AN INTRODUCTION AND NOTES BY
David Magarshack

London . Secker & Warburg

First published in England 1968 by
Martin Secker & Warburg Limited
14 Carlisle Street, London, W.1

Original title *Pis'ma k gruzinskim druz'jam*

The extract from *I Remember: Sketch for an Autobiography*,
translated by David Magarshack, is used by permission of
Pantheon Books, Inc.

SBN: 436 36350 X

Printed in Great Britain by
The Camelot Press Ltd., London and Southampton

Contents

CONTENTS

Illustrations

9

Introduction

Boris Pasternak's letters to his Georgian friends cover a period of twenty-eight years, from 1931 to 1959, years in which he had to battle against ever growing official hostility to his poetry which took the form of a ban on his books and forced him to take up translations as a way of earning a living. It was by sheer chance that he became a translator of Georgian poetry and it was this accident that, according to his fellow poet, Nikolai Tikhonov, was to be 'a turning point in his work' and, one might add, in his life. It was his newly-found friends, especially the poets Titian Tabidze and Paolo Yashvili, both of them victims of the purges of 1936–7, who, to quote Tikhonov again, 'surrounded him with such warm friendship and friendly sympathy that this first indelible impression remained with him throughout his life'. Pasternak himself was to describe Georgia as a country 'which has become my second motherland' and his Georgian friends as 'people whom I love like brothers'. It is this deeply emotional attitude towards his friendship with some of the most prominent Georgian poets that immediately strikes the reader of these letters. But it is also this aspect of his ties with Georgia that lays bare not only the personal feelings of a poet who was one of the most reserved and reticent of men imaginable, but also his views on the grimmest period of suppression and persecution which the liberal arts in Russia ever experienced. Of the sixty-seven letters in this volume, twenty-eight are addressed to Nina Tabidze after the arrest and presumed execution of her husband, Titian Tabidze. It is these letters that plumb the depths of Pasternak's emotional life and reveal his character as perhaps none of his autobiographical sketches does. The letters to Titian Tabidze and to the other Georgian poets contain further invaluable information about his personal life as well as about his views on poetry in general and his own poetry in particular. They also deal with the problems of translating poetry, especially from a language unfamiliar to the translator, who is forced to use interlinear translations and notes supplied by the poets themselves.

As with Georgian poetry, chance also played some part in Pasternak's choice of poetry as a career.

Born in Moscow in 1890, the son of Leonid Pasternak, a fashionable painter, and Rosa Pasternak, *née* Kaufmann, a concert pianist, Pasternak received the usual education of a son of a well-to-do professional family. He was educated at a Moscow secondary school and after meeting Alexander Scriabin at the age of twelve in the spring of 1903 was so carried away by Scriabin's 'freshness of spirit' that he decided to become a musician and devoted the next six years of his life to a thorough study of the theory of composition.

He soon realised that he could never be a success as a composer. He could scarcely play the piano and could not even read music with any fluency. He was then and till much later convinced that everything in art must be a miracle and nothing must be deliberately designed or planned. Inclined to mysticism and superstition from early childhood, he believed that everything must be predestined from above. He soon found, however, that so far as music was concerned, the discrepancy between his idea of creative art and the inadequacies of his musical technique made him completely unfit for the role of a successor to Scriabin. When that flamboyant composer returned to Russia with the score of his famous *Poem of Ecstasy*, Pasternak decided to give up his musical ambitions in spite of Scriabin's encouragement. In 1908 he joined the faculty of law at Moscow University and, on Scriabin's advice a year later, changed to the faculty of philosophy. In 1912 he continued his study of philosophy at Marburg University (he had visited Germany for the first time in 1906 with his family). By that time he had become a member of an *avant-garde* group of writers, poets and critics. After an abortive love affair he decided to give up philosophy and devote himself to poetry. On graduating from Moscow University, he wrote his first volume of poems, which he entitled 'with quite stupid pretentiousness', as he was to admit many years later, *A Twin in the Clouds*, 'in imitation of the cosmological ingenuities characteristic of the book titles of the symbolists'. In those poems, he declared in his *Sketch for an Autobiography* (1959), he 'did not express, reflect, represent or depict anything at all'. Later he confessed that he was often sorry to have published such 'an immature book'. In the spring of 1914 he joined the Centrifuge Futurist Association and in the same year, during one of the frequent clashes between warring groups of *avant-garde* poets, he met Mayakovsky. He finally broke with Mayakovsky in 1920, because he was unable to stomach Mayakovsky's 'clumsily rhymed sermons, his cultivated insipidity, his commonplaces and platitudes which were so artificial, confused, and devoid of humour'.

From the very beginning of his career as a poet Pasternak found it difficult to support himself by his writing. Between 1914 and 1916 he was tutor to the son of a Moscow industrialist and spent two winters (1916–17) doing clerical work in ordnance factories in the Urals. On his return to Moscow in March 1917 he published his second volume of poems, *Above the Barriers*, and his third volume, *My Sister, Life* in the summer of that year. His fourth volume of verse, *Themes and Variations*, was published in 1924. Pasternak was later to repudiate his early poems. He explains the reason for this repudiation in a letter to Simon Chikovani on 6 October 1957. In those poems, he wrote, he put down 'only what seemed to escape him by the character of the language or the turn of phrase of its own accord, involuntary and indivisible, unexpectedly right'. His main concern was not to make a poem as perfect as possible, but to make sure that at least some part of it 'came out red-hot and at a bound and owed its freshness and naturalness either to that fact or to chance and luck'.

His first prose works, *The Childhood of Luverse* and *Letters from Tula*, were written in 1918. His first marriage took place in 1922, in which year he left with his wife for Berlin to see his parents who had emigrated from the Soviet Union. After revisiting Marburg, he returned to Moscow in the autumn. Although now the author of several volumes of verse and prose, Pasternak's income from his own works was negligible —that was to be the recurrent trouble throughout his life, though it was not the obscurity of his poetry that was the cause of it later on but what he himself described in a letter to his closest friend Nina Tabidze, the wife of the Georgian poet, on 17 January 1953 as 'the obstructions caused by the events of our time'. In 1921 he obtained work as a salesman in the Writers' Bookshop in Moscow and in 1924 he worked in the Library of the People's Commissariat of Foreign Affairs. In 1925 he attempted, again unsuccessfully, to woo the reading public by publishing four short stories in book form: *Childhood of Luverse*, *Letters from Tula*, *Il Tratto di Apelle* and *Aerial Ways*. In

1927, however, he succeeded in getting the authorities to take a less obstructive attitude towards his poetry by his publication of two revolutionary poems: *The Year 1905* and *Lieutenant Schmidt* (of *Potemkin* fame). But the control over literature exercised by the Russian Association of Proletarian Writers (RAPP) from 1928 to 1932 put further obstacles in Pasternak's literary path, leaving him with the dubious reputation of a poet's poet. But again chance intervened and opened up for Pasternak, at the age of forty, a new literary career that was to provide him with a living for the rest of his life—the career of a translator.

Pasternak first met the Georgian poet Paolo Yashvili, one of the founders of the symbolist movement in Georgia, in Moscow in 1930, the year in which *Safe Conduct*, Pasternak's first autobiography, was being serialised in a Moscow literary magazine and in which Mayakovsky committed suicide, chiefly, it would seem, because he could no longer bring himself to toe the line laid down by RAPP. Pasternak was afterwards to describe Yashvili as a brilliant man of the world, a cultured and entertaining conversationalist and a 'European' in every sense of the word. Soon after his visit, Yashvili was to become one of his closest friends. In his moving letter to Yashvili's wife after Yashvili's suicide in 1937 during the terrible year of the Stalin purges, Pasternak recalls Yashvili's 'striking face with its high, inspired forehead and laughing eyes' and the sound of his voice 'that was so fascinating from its overflow of ideas'. Yashvili was to come to his rescue at a critical period of his life. For in 1930 his first marriage foundered and, in the changes that took place in his family and in the family of the woman he had fallen in love with, the two of them for some time had, as Pasternak expressed it, 'no roof over our heads'. They took refuge in Yashvili's house in Tiflis (Tbilisi). On the day of their arrival, Yashvili introduced Pasternak to the members of the group of Georgian poets whose leader he was, including the man who was to become his other great friend—Titian Tabidze.

Pasternak had never been to Georgia before and the Caucasus and the life of the Georgian people were a complete revelation to him. He admired the dark overhanging cliffs towering over all the streets of the city. He found the life of the ordinary, and particularly the poorest, inhabitants much brighter, more candid and much less inhibited than in the north. The educated classes of the population showed, in his view, a higher level of intellectual life than he was used to in Moscow. The fine buildings in certain quarters of Tiflis reminded him of Petersburg. The city was full of picturesque lanes. There was the continuous sound of popular Georgian folk music: tambourines, bagpipes and other national instruments. He was fascinated by the brightness of the stars in the sky at night and the scent of the flowers from innumerable gardens mingling with the smells issuing from coffee-houses and confectioners' shops. But the spell the southern city cast on him was nothing compared to the spell cast by the two poets who were to become his closest friends and whose lives were to end so tragically six years later—Paolo Yashvili and Titian Tabidze.

Both, he was later to declare, became an integral part of his personal life. They were inseparable and complementary. Yashvili was turned outwards. His poetry was constructed on exact data and the evidence of his senses. Tabidze, who was thirty-six when Pasternak, who was five years his senior, met him, was turned inwards and all he wrote came from the depths of his inner self.

During Tabidze's life Pasternak did not quite realise how close the bond was that linked him to 'the thickset, compact figure of the smiling poet'. It was only after Tabidze's arrest and execution in 1937 that Tabidze's real place in his life became clear to him. It was not a feeling, he wrote to Nina Tabidze, it was 'a magical fact'.

During Pasternak's next visit to Georgia, he met a number of other Georgian poets, including Georgy (Gogla) Leonidze, whose poems he would be occupied in translating between the years 1932 and 1943, a period almost entirely devoted to translations. In 1931 he had published his novel in verse, *Spectorsky*, a collection of children's poems, *The Zoo*, and a volume of collected poems, *The Second Birth*.

It was in November 1933 that Pasternak arrived in Georgia with members of the committee supervising the organisation of the First Congress of Soviet Writers (a reference to it will be found in his letter to Nina and Titian Tabidze of 6 November 1933). Among the other members were Nikolai Tikhonov and Victor Goltsev. It was during this visit that Pasternak and Tikhonov undertook a vast programme of translations of Georgian poetry. In 1935 the publishing house 'Soviet Writer' issued a volume of Pasternak's translations of Georgian poems under the title *Georgian Lyrics*. In Tiflis a volume of translations by Pasternak and Tikhonov under the title *Poets of Georgia* was published in the same year.

In 1934, Pasternak's translation of Vazha Pshavela's narrative poem *Zmeyeyed* (The Serpent Eater) was published in a separate edition. In 1940 Pasternak translated two poems by Tsereteli and in 1945 took an active part in the celebration of the jubilee of N. Baratashvili by translating almost all of his poems. In the thirties Pasternak translated, in addition to the above classics of Georgian poetry, poems by Abasheli, Abashidze, Gaprindashvili, Grishashvili, Kaladze, Leonidze, Mashashvili, Nadiradze, Chikovani and Yashvili. In a speech at one of the plenary sessions of the Union of Soviet Writers, Pasternak declared: 'I must state in all frankness that for me the work of translating Georgian poetry was a piece of good fortune. This work exerted a most happy influence on my creative work.'

His Georgian experiences left their mark on some of the more important cycles of Pasternak's poems, including *The Second Birth*, *Travel Notes* (summer, 1936), and *The Artist* (winter, 1936).

A key to the understanding of the poetry of Pasternak's correspondents and the works of the Georgian poets he translated, which are mentioned in his letters, is provided by the following, hitherto unpublished, essay on *The New Georgian Poetry* which Pasternak intended as an introduction to his volume of translations published in 1946 in Tiflis under the title of *Georgian Poets*:

Modern Georgian poetry occupies a prominent place in the Georgian arts. It owes its vitality and vividness to some extent to the treasures of the Georgian language. Georgian colloquial speech is still permeated by survivals of old sayings and traces of forgotten popular beliefs. Many Georgian idioms owe their origin to the ritualistic peculiarities of the ancient pagan and new Christian calendars. The beauties of some saying or subtlety of some proverb, for instance, more than ritual Byzantine chants or church frescoes, arise from the sensitiveness and vivacity of the Georgian character, an inclination to give free rein to the imagination, an oratorical vein, an ability to be carried away.

These features of conviviality and buffoonery form the essence of the genius and nature of Nikolai Baratashvili. Like a meteor, he illuminated Georgian poetry for a century ahead and laid down a path which has remained indelible to this day.

In spite of his personal unsociability and the loneliness of his Muse, Baratashvili cannot be imagined in the silence of real seclusion for which he sighs so often. He cannot be separated from urban society, with which he is always at daggers drawn, as a ray of light is inseparable from the facet of a crystal which splits it up and forms a rainbow at the point of its break-up. The tragic conflicts of Baratashvili with his environment are so simply and clearly explained by him that they have become a school of love of peace and loyalty to society for posterity.

Nearest and equal to him in significance is Vazha Pshavela, who is in many ways his complete opposite.

Firstly, in contrast to Baratashvili, Vazha Pshavela is a genuine recluse and contemplator lost in inaccessible mountains. Besides, only death the pacifier fused Baratashvili's original diction with colloquial speech, while from the very beginning Vazha Pshavela wrote as the common people speak in the mountains under the burden of their everyday life. However, this austere note of dissociation of the high mountain dweller Vazha Pshavela deepened to such an extent that his books became the property also of the chosen few and a religion of personality capable of holding its own with the creations of the West's great individualists of today.

The poetic literature of our time in any country of the world, including Russia and Georgia, is the natural result of the symbolist movement and all its followers as well as of all the schools that were hostile to it. The consummation of all these movements can be taken to be the fresh, diverse and original work of Simon Chikovani.

He earned the right to that place by the definitiveness and finality of his tone—the usual characteristic of everything great as distinct from diffuse approximation—the mark of anything which is less than perfect.

The figurative element, common to all poetry, assumes in Chikovani a new, modified, heightened, and essential significance. Chikovani is by nature an artist and painter, and it is this artistic quality of his, of the order of Whitman and Verhaeren, which lends breadth and freedom to his choice of themes and their treatment.

In poetry the image is hardly ever only visual, but represents a composite image of life, compounded of the testimonies of our senses and all the aspects of our consciousness. In conformity with this, the pictorial imagery, which we spoke of in connection with Chikovani, is far from mere representation. It is the highest degree of embodiment and signifies the maximum and final concreteness of everything as a whole: of any idea, of any theme, of any emotion, of any observation.

Chikovani is not an accidental but a natural link in the general development of Georgian thought. He combines the fairy-tale ingenuity of Vazha Pshavela with the impetuous, completely manifest, dramatic quality of Baratashvili.

We would greatly distort the picture of the modern condition of Georgian poetry if we passed over in silence another remarkable and vivid talent of our times—Georgy Leonidze, a poet of concentrated and rare moods, which cannot be separated from the soil on which they were born or from the language in which they are expressed. He is the author of model poems, almost untranslatable into any other language. But our remarks do not claim to be exhaustive, or we should not have overlooked the literary work and fame of Akaky Tsereteli, the fresh and gripping spontaneity of Nikolai Nadiradze, the great craftsmanship of Valerian Gaprindashvili and many others.

Still more confused and unsystematic than our remarks are our haphazard selections. There is, for instance, the glaring omission of Tabidze's *Galaktion*, justly the pride of contemporary Georgian poetic literature, and insufficient acquaintance with another of its ornaments, Josif Grishashvili, represented in this volume by one poem only. . . .

The first years of my acquaintance with Georgian lyrical poetry are a special, bright and unforgettable page of my life. The memories of the incitements and incentives which gave rise to these translations as well as the details of the surroundings in which they were produced, have merged into a whole world, distant and precious. . . .

But that page was soon to be stained with blood. The relaxation of the strict surveillance over the works of Russian writers which followed the dissolution of RAPP in 1932 was soon to be followed by the horror of the mass trials and indiscriminate executions of 1936–7, in which Pasternak's closest friends, Tabidze and Yashvili, were to perish. Pasternak himself had only just returned from a journey to Paris where he had attended the first anti-fascist congress and where he had met Marina Tsvetaeva, the poet he so greatly admired. On his return to Russia he fell seriously ill after a heart attack. He mentions his illness and his 'numerous and aimless absences' in convalescent homes in his letter to Tabidze of 6 October 1935. How little he realised the danger threatening Tabidze and numerous other writers and poets can be gathered from the letter he wrote on 8 April 1936 to Tabidze at the time of the most acrimonious debate in the general and literary press about 'formalism'. In it he urged Tabidze not to be influenced by the facile arguments of the official Soviet press and the Union of Soviet Writers, but to follow 'the new promptings' of his own heart. 'You need not worry,' he wrote. 'I am not the only one who appreciates you and believes in you.' He therefore urged Tabidze to reject 'the critical semolina porridge' advocated by the Soviet authorities and to believe in himself, in his own 'line' and not in the Party line. Little did he dream that that was exactly the reason why Beria, who had been put in charge of the purges in Georgia, should have chosen as one of his first victims Titian Tabidze, the man Pasternak characterised in his autobiographical essay as 'a reserved and complicated soul, wholly attracted to the good and capable of clairvoyance and self-sacrifice'. Paolo Yashvili, horrified at the news of Tabidze's arrest and execution and perhaps fearing the same fate, went to the headquarters of the Union of Georgian Writers, of which he was secretary, and blew out his brains with the shot from his double-barrelled gun. One of the most moving and deeply felt letters in this volume is the one Pasternak sent to Yashvili's widow on 28 August 1937, in which he describes the shock he felt at the news of Yashvili's suicide and his personal feeling of great loss as he realised that he would never again 'see that wonderful face with its high, inspired forehead and laughing eyes and never hear the voice whose very sound was fascinating . . .'. He forecast that Yashvili would become the Georgian Mayakovsky and that the future Georgian literature, 'if,' he added, for once openly expressing his dismay at the slaughter of so many promising young writers, 'it is destined to develop', would emulate and study him.

Tabidze's fate was still unknown at the time. Only seventeen years later the first secretary of the Georgian Communist Party, in announcing the rehabilitation of many Georgian writers and scientists at the Congress of the Union of Georgian Writers in July 1954 disclosed that such 'outstanding masters of the Georgian language' as 'Titian Tabidze and Paolo Yashvili became the victims of the intrigues and terrorism of that abominable gang of murderers'. But even then Nina Tabidze and Pasternak did not give up hope that Tabidze might still be alive in some Siberian forced labour camp. It was only in October 1955 that Tabidze's execution two months after his arrest in the summer of 1937 was finally confirmed. 'I always sensed this terrible truth,' Pasternak wrote to Nina Tabidze on

4 October 1955. 'It determined my views, my attitude towards the time we live in and' (another important confession which under any other circumstances would never have escaped him), 'its chief representatives, and my future. Poor, poor Tabidze who had to suffer this martyrdom!' At first Pasternak did his best not to shatter Nina Tabidze's hopes of a possible reunion with her husband. In a letter he wrote to her in 1938 and in all his subsequent letters to her, he encouraged her 'to live in hope'. In 1938 he wrote to her: 'Last winter when it was all connected *only* with horror and suffering, I sometimes woke up in tears, thinking that what pained me was not my pain, but that I had become part of your own terrible shock and a part of yourself and that is why it was so intense.' As for his own position, he confessed that he found things 'a little more difficult'. He thought it was his own fault, for, he added drily, 'I was never very good at enthusiasm. During the last two years it became more than I could bear . . .'. His financial position, never too brilliant, suffered greatly as a result of the purges: 'Nobody signs big contracts with me,' he told Nina Tabidze in the same letter.

But he went on with his translations of the Georgian poets and Shakespeare. In his letter to Nina Tabidze of 24 November 1940 he mentioned that his translation of *Hamlet* was to be performed by the Moscow Art Theatre, and in another letter to her, on 6 February 1941, he enquired anxiously whether the Russian theatre in Tiflis intended to go on with their promised production of his translation of *Hamlet*.

Except for a vague hint in his letter to Leonidze on 20 May 1941, exactly a month before the German invasion of Russia, no mention of the war in Europe occurs in Pasternak's letters to his Georgian friends. On the outbreak of the war Pasternak, together with other Russian writers, was evacuated to Chistopol, a town on the Kama, in the Tatar region ('I lived there in

1915,' Pasternak reminded Nina Tabidze in his letter of 20 March 1942; 'all my Kamas and Urals were quite near'). In Yelabug, a neighbouring town on the Kama, Marina Tsvetaeva hanged herself in the autumn of 1941. 'A poet of great potentialities,' Pasternak described her in the same letter. He was back in Moscow at the time, but he felt that he was to a certain extent to blame for her suicide, for he should have realised how desperate her situation was and should have taken steps to help her. In December 1942, he wrote his poem *To the Memory of Marina Tsvetaeva*, in which he expressed the hope of transferring her remains from 'godforsaken Yelabug' to Moscow.

Early in the war Pasternak tried to obtain permission to go to the front as war correspondent. In a letter to his wife, who had been evacuated to Chistopol with the children, Pasternak wrote in November 1942: 'I asked Fadeyev to arrange for me to go to the front. He undertook to carry out my request with great enthusiasm, but, as you see, I am still in Moscow. Now I have sent the same request to the editorial office of *Krasnaya Zvezda* [Red Star] and I expect to be leaving for the front about the 20th . . .'.

At the beginning of December 1942 he wrote again: 'Three weeks ago I expressed the wish to go to the front to Fadeyev and *Krasnaya Zvezda*. They were so enthusiastic about it that I was afraid they would not give me half an hour for the necessary preparations. During the last two weeks I rang *Krasnaya Zvezda* every night (they work at night there) and every time I was told that I would be sent off shortly.' He had to wait another nine months before he was given permission to go. He left Moscow for the front in August 1943. His dispatches from the front first appeared in print in 1965, in the January number of *Novy Mir*.

During the war Pasternak published several patriotic war poems and continued his translations of Shakespeare. The ban

on his books had been somewhat relaxed and in 1943 he published his volume of poems, *In Early Trains*, and in 1945
another volume, *Wide Open Spaces*. But in August 1946 two
more sacrificial offerings were made on the altar of Soviet
literature. This followed Zhdanov's denunciation of Zoshchenko and the distinguished poet, Akhmatova. Zhdanov
described Akhmatova as 'not quite a nun, not quite a wanton,
but both a wanton and a nun' and her poetry as 'the poetry of
an agitated lady, tossing between the boudoir and the chapel'.
Zhdanov's denunciation followed the condemnation by the
Central Committee of contributions by Zoshchenko and
Akhmatova in two Leningrad literary journals. One can only
presume that Pasternak escaped the same fate because he did not
happen to have published anything at the time. The only
oblique reference to these events can be found in his letter to
Nina Tabidze on 22 December 1946, in which he tried to
assure her that all was well with him. 'I suppose, one must not
complain', he writes, 'or, perhaps one must—I find it difficult to
judge, so blinded am I by the inner happiness of my existence.
. . . But why, why do I feel so well in this world? I am ready
to weep—it is so startling and inexplicable.' It might to some
extent be explained by the supposition that, unlike Akhmatova,
he had escaped being expelled from the Union of Soviet Writers
though, as a result of Zhdanov's attack on 'cosmopolitanism'
in Soviet literature, he was completely silenced. But four years
later (Zhdanov being safely dead by that time), the ban on
Akhmatova was lifted. 'You must already have seen Akhmatova's poems in *Ogonyok*,' Pasternak wrote to Nina Tabidze on
6 April 1950, 'or heard about their publication. . . . I am terribly
glad of this literary sensation and this event in her life, and the
only thing that is unpleasant is that by the same token they have
all started looking expectantly in my direction.' In the same
year, as if to justify the expectancy of his friends, his translation

of Goethe's *Faust* was published and later the periodical *Znamya* published ten poems from *Doctor Zhivago*, one of which, *Star of the Nativity*, he sent to Simon Chikovani's wife on 25 February 1947. There are several references to *Doctor Zhivago* in his Georgian letters. It was while working on his novel that he wrote to Nina Tabidze on 6 April 1950: 'I am very satisfied with my life, with a chance of earning an honest living, and with the serenity of my state of mind. I have never considered myself in any way offended or passed over. If anyone thinks that to a detached observer I may appear to be a "martyr", then let me say that, first, I am not responsible for anyone's crazy ideas or ridiculous fancies and, secondly, it is sufficient that they who may be interested in such a theory should lift the ban on my books and let me mount the rostrum and this semblance of martyrdom which *does not exist* will disappear by itself.' But *they* did not lift the ban. On the contrary, when he submitted the manuscript of *Doctor Zhivago* to the editorial board of *Novy Mir* it was rejected in September 1956. He might have expected this from the reaction of some of his friends who had read his novel in the spring of 1952. 'Of those who read my novel,' he wrote to the Chikovanis in April 1952, 'the majority are dissatisfied. They say it is a failure and that they expected more from me, that it is colourless, that it is not worthy of me, but, acknowledging all this, I just grin as though this abuse and condemnation were praise.' What he did not apparently expect was the fury of vituperation and abuse let loose on him in the Soviet press after the publication of translations of *Doctor Zhivago* in Italy in 1957 and in England and the United States in 1958. After his award of the Nobel Prize for Literature, he was at last expelled from the Union of Soviet Writers on 27 October 1958. He had already had several heart attacks during the last fifteen years of his life (a very serious one in January 1953, described in one of the finest letters he wrote to Nina Tabidze on 17 January 1953), and his expulsion and the continuing violent attacks on him aggravated his condition. 'It is most probable,' he wrote after leaving hospital in May 1958 to the editor of the last edition of his *Poems about Georgia* and *Georgian Poets*, 'that only many years after my death will it become clear what were the reasons, the great, the overwhelmingly great reasons, that lay at the foundation of the activity of my last years, the air it breathed and drew sustenance from, what it served.' The hounding of Pasternak inevitably resulted in a disastrous fall in the sale of his published books as can be gathered from his letter to one of the directors of a Tiflis publishing house on 2 September 1958. 'Though I am forgotten to the point of complete obscurity,' he wrote, 'I did not think I had been forgotten so completely that my book would not go through at least ten editions, which would have covered your expenses and the cost of publication. I realise that it does not of course depend on you, for people in high office keep interfering with the future of literature; however, the rest are only too willing to follow them.'

In March 1959 Pasternak and his wife paid a last visit to Georgia. They spent three weeks as guests of Nina Tabidze who, Pasternak wrote on 17 March 1959, to one of his Georgian friends, 'showered love, care, comfort and repose upon us'. He did not think he would ever again experience 'anything more radiant' in his life. On his return 'portents of dangers and sufferings' awaited him, but, he added with his usual stoic acceptance of whatever misfortune befell him throughout his life, 'everywhere in the world one has to pay for the right to live on one's own naked spiritual reserves'. It was his last letter to his Georgian friends. He died on 30 May 1960.

D. M.

From Boris Pasternak's
I Remember

During the decades since the publication of *Safe Conduct*, I often thought that if I were to republish it I would add a chapter on the Caucasus and two Georgian poets. Time passed and the need for other additions did not arise. The only gap that remained was this missing chapter. I am going to write it now.

About 1930, in winter, Paolo Yashvili and his wife paid me a visit in Moscow. Yashvili was a brilliant man of the world, a cultured and entertaining conversationalist, a 'European', a tall and handsome man.

Soon after their visit all sorts of upheavals, complications, and changes took place in two families, that of a friend of mine and my own. They were very painful to those implicated in them. For some time my companion, who was afterwards to become my second wife, and I had no roof over our heads. Yashvili offered us a place of refuge at his house in Tiflis.

At that time the Caucasus, Georgia, the life of the Georgian people and some of its individual representatives were a complete revelation to me. Everything was new, everything was surprising. Dark bulks of overhanging mountains towered at the end of all the street vistas of Tiflis. The life of the city's poorest inhabitants, brought out from the yards into the streets, was bolder and less concealed than in the North. It was brighter and more candid. It was full of mysticism and the messianic symbolism of folk legends which are so favourable to the life of the imagination and which, as in Catholic Poland, turn every man into a poet. The more advanced section of the population showed a high level of cultural and intellectual life that was seldom to be met with in those days. The fine buildings of certain parts of Tiflis reminded me of Petersburg; some had railings outside the first-floor windows which were bent in the shape of baskets or lyres. The city also abounded in picturesque back lanes. Big tambourines beating to the rhythm of the *lezginka* followed you about everywhere and always seemed to catch up with you. In addition, there were the goat-like bleatings of the bagpipes and some other musical instruments. Nightfall in a Southern town was full of stars and the scent of flowers from the gardens mingled with the smells from coffeehouses and confectioners' shops.

Paolo Yashvili is a remarkable poet of the post-symbolist period. His poetry is constructed on exact data and the evidence of the senses. It is akin to the modern European prose of Bely, Hamsun, and Proust and, like that prose, is fresh with unexpected and accurate observations. It is creative poetry *par excellence*. It is not cluttered up with tightly crammed effects. It is spacious and airy. It moves and breathes.

The First World War caught Yashvili in Paris. He was a student at the Sorbonne. He returned to his native country by a roundabout route. At a remote Norwegian railway station, Yashvili, lost in a daydream, did not notice that his train had left. A young Norwegian married couple, a farmer and his wife, who had come by sledge from their remote village for the post, saw the daydreaming, fiery Southerner and the unfortunate result of his daydreams. They were sorry for Yashvili and, after succeeding somehow or other in making themselves understood, took him with them to their farm where he was to stay till the next train which was only expected in two days' time.

Yashvili was a marvellous raconteur. He was a born teller of adventure stories. He was always beset by the sort of surprises that one only reads about in novels. Chance played a prominent part in his life. He had a gift for it. He was lucky that way.

In his company one could not help feeling that one was in the presence of a highly gifted man. His eyes blazed with the fire of his soul, his lips were seared by the fire of his passions. His face was scorched and blackened by the heat of experience, so that he seemed to be older than his age, a man who had been through a great deal, a man who was a little the worse for wear.

On the day of our arrival he collected his friends, the members of the group whose leader he was. I don't remember who came on that occasion. His next-door neighbour, Nikolai Nadiradze, must quite certainly have been there. Titian Tabidze was there too with his wife.

I can see that room just as if I were there now. And how could I forget it? On that very evening, without suspecting the horrors that lay in store for it, I lowered it very gently so that it should not get broken to the bottom of my soul with all the terrible things that happened in it and near it.

Why were those two men sent to me? How shall I describe our relations? Both became integral parts of my personal world. I did not prefer one to the other because they were inseparable and complementary to one another. The fate of these two men, and that of Marina Tsvetaeva, was to become my greatest sorrow.

If Yashvili was turned outwards, all in a centrifugal direction, Titian Tabidze was turned inwards and every line he wrote and every step he took called you into the depths of his rich soul, so full of intuitions and forebodings.

The main thing in his poetry is the feeling of an inexhaustible fund of lyrical potentialities that is implied in every one of his poems, the preponderance of unsaid things and of those he would still say over those he had said already. This presence of an untouched store of spiritual reserves creates the background and lends depth to his poems and imparts that special mood with which they are imbued and which constitutes their principal and bitter charm. There is as much soul in his poems as there was in himself, a complex, esoteric soul, directed wholly towards good, capable of clairvoyance and self-sacrifice.

When I think of Yashvili all sorts of urban scenes come to my mind, rooms, arguments, addresses delivered at public meetings, Yashvili's dazzling eloquence at crowded parties at night.

The thought of Tabidze brings to mind the elements of nature, in my imagination arise all sorts of country scenes, the freedom of flowering meadows, the waves of the sea.

Clouds are sailing along, and in the distance, in a line with them, mountains rise up. And the thickset, compact figure of the smiling poet merges with them. He has a somewhat wavering gait. He shakes all over when he laughs. Now he gets up, stands sideways to the table, and taps his glass with a knife before making a speech. His habit of raising one shoulder higher than the other makes him look a little crooked.

His house in Kodzhary stands at the bend of the road. The road rises along the front and then, bending round the house, goes past its back wall. From that house one can see those who walk and those who drive past it twice.

It was at the height of the period when, according to Bely's witty definition, the triumph of materialism had abolished matter. There was nothing to eat; there was nothing to wear. There was nothing tangible around, only ideas. If we kept alive, it was thanks to our Tiflis friends, miracle workers who all the time managed to get something and bring something and provide us with advances from publishing houses for something we had no idea of.

We met, exchanged news, dined, read something to each other. The light, cool breezes played, as though with fingers, with the poplar's silvery foliage, velvety and white on the underside. The air, as with rumours, was full of the heavy scents of the South. Like the front of a cart on its coupling-pole, the night on high slowly turned the whole body of its starry chariot. And on the road bullock-carts and automobiles drove and moved along and every one of them could be seen from the house twice.

Or we were on the Georgian military road, or in Borzhom, or in Abastuman. Or after trips into the countryside, to beauty spots, adventures, and libations, we, each one of us with something or other, and I with a black eye from a fall, stopped in Bakuriany at the house of Leonidze, a most original poet, more than anyone else closely bound up with the mysteries of the language in which he wrote, and for that reason least of all amenable to translation.

A midnight feast on the grass in a wood, a beautiful hostess, two charming little daughters. Next day the unexpected arrival of a *mestvir*, a wandering minstrel with a bagpipe, and an impromptu glorification of everyone at the table in turn, with an appropriate text and an ability to seize on any excuse, like my black eye, for instance, for a toast.

Or we went to the seaside in Kabuleti. Rains and storms. In the same hotel Simon Chikovani, the future master of bright, picturesque verse, at the time still a member of the Communist Youth League. And above the line of all the mountains and horizons, the head of the smiling poet walking beside me, and the bright, luminous signs of his prodigious talent, and the shadow of sadness and destiny in his smile. And once more I bid farewell to him now on these pages. Let me, in his person, bid farewell to all my other memories.

Letters to Georgian Friends

1931

To Titian and Nina Tabidze

13 December 1931

Dear Titian Tabidze and Nina Alexandrovna,

Greetings, greetings to both of you, greetings and congratulations on your impending victory on the housing front. Dear Titian, however much I ought to be glad for you (you did greatly miss Tiflis and your family, didn't you?), I feel sad without you. Georgy Ivanovich Chulkov is about to leave on a visit to E. E. Lanseret and asked for your address. I gave it to him without obtaining you permission. I expect he will pay you a visit and give you our regards. Elena Mikhailovna Tager informs us that both of you and *you especially* (I even tried to convince her of the great merits of Paolo)[1] left your Petersburg friends completely enchanted and they kept recalling the party and yourselves long afterwards. After your departure a sort of week of Georgian poetry opened in Leningrad. You were understood and greatly appreciated—correctly characterised. During the debate that followed the address by Aseyev, Paolo spoke with more clarity and boldness than anyone—that is the

[1] Paolo Yashvili.

37

general opinion. I was late, missed the address, came towards the end and made the mistake of availing myself of the first opportunity of taking the floor. Not having heard the address, I had nothing to push off from and, I am told, I was not like you, but like the imitation Nitochka[1] gives of you. They understood nothing, they applauded, they forgave me. Now we are off again to the continuation of the debate. Perhaps I'll make amends and rehabilitate myself. I embrace you. Greetings to everybody.

Zina[2] kisses Nina Alexandrovna and sends her regards to you.

[1] Nitochka—Tanit Tabidze, daughter of Titian and Nina Tabidze.
[2] Zina—Zinaida Nikolaevna Pasternak.

1932

---

30 July 1932

My dear, dear Paolo,

Weeks pass, adding up to months, and if we were to go on like this, you would never realise that the moment I took up my quarters here at the lakeside I began to write to you. I began several letters to you and left them unfinished, one after the other, because of their length. They took the form of researches into the history of the Urals or attempts to tell you (!) what is Georgia.

The remarkable thing is that we had barely settled here when for the second time we began to live through the summer we had spent with you. We never before experienced anything that took possession of our thoughts so powerfully and so entirely. We became aware of it on the very first morning as soon as we had woken up in our country cottage, consisting of three rooms and a veranda, which the Ural Regional Committee of the Communist Party put at our disposal. We went for a walk to the lake and on its opposite shore saw a forest stretching for a hundred miles, pines and birches, the mica-like

39

surface of the water, the clouds, the graves of the old church-yard, the familiar Northern gamut of impressions. We made no comparisons. As though with one accord, as though we had agreed to do so, we simply called out: Kodzhora, and then, with mounting consistency, began to recall Tiflis, Okrokhany, Kobulety, Tsagveri and Bakuriani, and all the places and their whereabouts. Today I saw Tezik in my mind's eye together with Tamara Alexandrovna[1]. Tomorrow someone else. I felt terribly happy for you, that you were there now, that you were again surrounded by it all, and that you would see them all.

For this is not only the South and the Caucasus, that is, beauty that is always unfathomable and everywhere over-whelming; and it is not only Titian and Shanshiashvili, Nadiradze and Mitsishvili, Gaprindashvili and Leonidze,[2] that is to say, remarkable men by any standards anywhere, men for whom one need not seek comparison to realise how incom-parable they are. It is something bigger, something, moreover, that has now become a rarity in the whole world. For (apart from its fairy-tale uniqueness) it is in more senses than one a country which has most astonishingly never experienced a break in its existence, a country which has remained down to earth even now and has not been carried off into a sphere of abstraction, a country of amaranthine colour and of everyday reality, however great its present hardships may be.

It was just in this light that we now began to see Georgia and

[1] T. A. Gruzinskaya and her son P. Gruzinsky—acquaintances of Paster-nak.

[2] Sandro Shanshiashvili (b. 1888), a Georgian poet and dramatist. The poets Kolau (Nikolai) Nadiradze (b. 1894), Valerian Gaprindashvili (1889–1941), Georgy Leonidze (1899–1966), the poet and prose writer Nikolai Mitsishvili (1896–1937) were for a time members of the group of Georgian symbolists 'Blue Horns', headed by Paolo Yashvili (1895–1937) and Titian Tabidze (1895–1937).

we could not help being amazed at the things we had experienced with you, as though it were something inconceivable and a legend. Why, I must have felt it when, confused and unable to find the right expressions, I spoke with Dzhavakhishvili[1] about Georgia as something unique. . . . It's clear to me now. That city [Tiflis] with all the people I saw in it and with all the things I had gone to experience and all the things I had brought with me will be the same to me as Chopin, Scriabin, Marburg, Venice and Rilke have been, one of the chapters of my *Safe Conduct*, which goes on all through my life, one of the chapters which, as you know, are not numerous; one of these chapters, and it will be the next to be written. I say 'will be' because I am a writer, and all this has to be written down and an expression found for it all; I say 'will be' because so far as I am concerned it has already become a fact.

That is why I keep writing one letter after another to you and destroying them one after another. This is no longer a matter of carrying on a free correspondence. This circle of memories has already taken possession of me: already *it* writes me, as Titian[2] would have said. It has already become independent of me, an experience discovered in a ready-made form, like a flowering plant, that is to say, it is capable of feeding on everything I am experiencing and will be experiencing after it; and until its place is taken by some new centre of the same kind, that is, until it is in its turn equal to Scriabin, Rilke, Venice and Tiflis, all the juices of the earth, gradually spread by the flow of time, will feed it. An example is not far to seek. I arrived in the Ural region, as I am beginning to see clearly now, for the sake of this experience, in the name of Tiflis. But it is difficult to write

[1] Mikhail Dzhavakhishvili (1880–1937), a Georgian prose writer.
[2] A reference to Titian Tabidze's lines:

> I do not write poems. Like a novel, they write
> Me, and the course of life accompanies them.

about all this in a letter, even if it is the fifth in number. It is not in a letter, of course, that all this will be expressed. Whatever I may happen to have in mind now, I shan't be able to ignore Georgia in my next work. And all this (what exactly, it is difficult to foresee) will be centred round your wonderful country, just as the story of a part of my life is focused on Mayakovsky.

Need I say after this how difficult I find it to realise in all its human vitality this self-enriching love of mine for you and everything yours, dividing it up among each of you, and addressing it to you and Titian, Titian and Nadiradze, and Nadiradze and Gaprindashvili. Such a correspondence, according to what I feel and what does not quit my imagination, ought to become my new vocation. And, yielding to impulse, I should not know where to stop. For, following the dictates of my heart, I should have had to write letters not only to Tamara Georgievna and Nina Alexandrovna, not only to Nitochka and Medea,[1] but also to the streets along which they walk, and the plane trees which cast their shade upon them. . . . Indeed, I should also have had to carry on a correspondence with the disappointments you cause them.

Please, kiss them all affectionately for me and tell all the places I have been to that they are the best and the most precious that the earth could have produced. And, please, tell one of these places that I who am about to sit down shortly to write some prose about all sorts of things, the North and the civil war, believe a little in the fulfilment of this decision only because I shall be writing about the Ural region while in my thoughts I shall be in Okrokhany and this will find its expression in my writing.

It is not inadvertently that I am not giving you my address. I should like very much to know how you are getting on and

[1] Medea, Paolo Yashvili's daughter.

what you are doing, you and your closest friends. But you would not reply and the longer you do not reply the more it will worry you. Well, be well and make the most of this ignorance of where to write to us. In the autumn, if you are not in Moscow by then, we shall resume our correspondence.

It is amazing that the man who was not there should have better understood a certain aspect of my feelings towards last summer. It is Robakidze.[1] However, in spite of my abiding inability to express the essence of what I feel without all sorts of complicating details, this peculiarity of mine will perhaps make some impression on you and Titian.

I embrace you warmly, and half of the letter is also written by Zina. Often also Adik[2] supplies proofs of the liveliness of his memory especially so far as the Caucasus is concerned. *Calamis tsveri*,[3] *calamis tsveri*, I say to him, and he springs to life suddenly and starts talking about the downpour of rain in Bakuriani.

Au revoir to all,

B. P.

[1] Grigory Robakidze (1884–1963), a writer close to the group 'Blue Horns', who subsequently emigrated.

[2] Adik—A. G. Neuhaus, Zina Pasternak's elder son by her first marriage.

[3] *Calamis tsveri* (Georgian)—the nib of a pen.

1933

To Besso A. Zhgenti[1]

6 October 1933

Dear Comrade Zhgenti,

   I have begun the translation of modern poets of Georgia. If you can make use of the enclosed four translations (three poems by Tabidze and one by P. Yashvili) for your journal *Literature and Art of Transcaucasia*, then by all means do so. If there should be any fee for them, send it to Titian for the repayment of the thousand roubles I borrowed from him two years ago and have not had time to return to him. I owe more money to Paolo, but I shall repay it by future publications. Comrade Besso, if the poems by Chikovani on Svaneti (there is one epic poem among them) have not yet been translated, ask him to get them ready for me to translate. Titian will explain how to prepare an interlinear translation (but with accents, which he does not indicate). My request for the preparation of the material refers not only to Chikovani, but to all the poets whose list you will draw up together with Titian and Chikovani. The book will contain no less than two thousand lines. Vazha Pshavela's

[1] A Georgian literary critic.

44

narrative poem, which will be the first in the book, will alone run to about one thousand lines. But I have only just begun translating it and I shall go on working on it at the same time as on my own prose. Here people are very interested in this collection of poems and Titian has made a terrific impression in the editorial offices of the Gorky almanac *Annual XVI*, in which his poems will be published. 'What a great poet you have discovered for us,' they said to me . . . Paolo's poem is shattering. I have read nothing more important or more vivid on Lenin's death. I press your hand warmly. All the best. Regards to our friends. Hurry up with your reply.

Yours,

B. Pasternak

To Titian Tabidze

12 October 1933

Dear Titian,

Thank you for your comments which reached me through Paolo and Eleuther.[1] I think I understand why they arrived by so circuitous a route and I'd like to thank you for this show of tact.

Do you really like my translations? You must forgive me if I doubt it: all translations—good and bad—are to a certain extent a violation of the original text, and mine, I'm afraid, are of the second category. I probably vulgarise you, for in the course of his work every artist forms his own idea of the substantiality

[1] E. L. Andronikashvili, a Georgian physicist, brother of the writer I. Andronikov.

of a word and mine is very rough: there is a great deal of dilettantism in it, which does not blend very well with life. In its banality it has not gone much beyond what is so character-istic of the poetry of Nadson, Apukhtin and Esenin, if one picks out the weakest points of these poets to define the shortcomings of other poets. I am well aware of it, but this is true not only of my translations of you and Paolo, but of my entire volume.

As for the inaccuracy which I permit myself in this work, my fault will perhaps be lessened to some extent if I entitle the volume: *From Georgian Poets*, that is, the emphasis in the title will shift from the claim of an exact rendering towards the indicated source from which these attempts originate. Given this unassuming title, my conscience will be absolutely clear. Annensky has a translation of Heine's *Ich grolle nicht*. There may be more accurate translations of Heine, but to my ear only this translation is alive and it seems accurate to me because I like it and, as with a living organism, it is different at different times, as is Heine's original, and this is what makes them so similar.

Be that as it may, you are very much liked here and you will be published in the third number of the almanac *Annual XVI*. I have not so far sent in Paolo's poems. I shall do so tomorrow without waiting for his elucidations of two or three passages, which I did not quite understand. But I could not get him on the telephone either yesterday or today and, if possible, I shall send his things to Zhgenti and hand them in to the editorial offices here with the above-mentioned uncorrected passages, which could be corrected in the galley proofs. If you see Zhgenti, tell him that I may want the proofs.

Do not be surprised, Titian, at some slight contrast between my first letter and this one: there is no discrepancy between them. The outburst of gratitude, which you aroused in me, did not remain without a sequel. The miracle of life remains in force, it does not cease for a moment, and binds me to you and Nina Alexandrovna with all the fibres of my being. Write to me at Volkhonka, 'pushing off' from the translation. Paolo and I arranged to arrive together at the end of the month, but I am beginning to be afraid of the frosts on the journey and I don't think I shall go after all. . . .

Your,

B. P.

To Titian Tabidze

23 October 1933

Dear Titian,

I shall not be able to leave with Paolo today as we planned. I shall, perhaps, arrive with the group which is setting off for Tiflis at the beginning of November, but that, too, is still uncertain. Meanwhile, I have signed the contract for the volume of translations, as I have perhaps written to you already.

I am beginning to be seriously alarmed about the fate of that book. I have to send it in at the end of January, and I would have easily coped with the work, if I had known the language and did not have to ask for help from the people I am translating.

Paolo was very busy here and could give me only an insignificant part of what I had asked him. He began to do a prose translation of Vazha Pshavela's *Zmeyeyed*, but could not finish it. Apart from what I sent to Zhgenti, I could get nothing from Paolo, and I do not blame him, so busy was he with his own affairs. . . .

I had wanted to translate Vazha Pshavela, Paolo, you Gaprindashvili, Leonidze, Nadiradze (Mitsishvili, if he writes poetry), Chikovani and also give translations from Tabidze's *Galaktion* and Grishashvili. Moreover, Paolo advised me to add to them Shanshiashvili, Abasheli, Lordkipanidze, Kaladze and Mashashvili. They must send me interlinear translations and that as soon as possible. All this has to reach me in the course of November. Anything sent later than that I shall not be able to translate because of my contract. But I am reluctant to impose on anyone and it is you in particular that I trust in this business, that is, I ask you to help me in obtaining interlinear translations, but only from those I have enumerated, who will do it easily and willingly. You, Titian, know the kind of interlinear translations I want. Though there are no accents in Georgian, I'd very much like them to indicate, even by conventional signs, how exactly the poem is read. For instance, I never heard people pronounce Tábidze or Tabidzé, but always Tabídze. Thus you read: *léksebi* and not *leksébi* or *leksebí*. . . . Let me put it another way. Just place yourself in the position of a Russian translator and, in conformity with your knowledge of the Russian language and verse, give him clear indications for the reproduction of the metre. Otherwise it becomes a matter of arbitrary decisions, as it was in relation to Paolo and yourself, however much Paolo tries to convince me to the contrary, i.e. that the metre has been piously observed. I merely reproduced the idea of the metre as I heard it, for you and Paolo once read those things to me and I had something to go on, which I shall not have in other cases.

Dear Titian, this request is addressed to you. Give me a few more poems, only a few have been translated. As for the other names, I am unable to address myself to the authors directly (except for Gaprindashvili, Nadiradze and Leonidze), help me with this either directly or through Zhgenti.

To Titian and Nina Tabidze

6 November 1933

My dear friends Nina Alexandrovna and Titian,

I do not know the name of the hill from which the Tiflis trains depart. It could be seen from our window in Oriante.[1] I often looked at it as I watched the slowly drifting smoke disappearing behind the projecting rocks and then reappearing again. I, too, began to carry out the same manœuvres as the smoke when you and the Korneyevs[2] disappeared round the bend and Nikolai[3] and Goltsev could, had they wished, by watching the clock from the window of the hotel have calculated how slow was my leave-taking of the wonderful city, how many of its glimpses from behind the rocks I thought to be the last and final ones, after which it appeared again, as though looking back out of what already seemed to be the impossible and beyond expectation, and how hard I found it after all this to keep back my tears.

Happy, happy ones! How gladly I'd have exchanged your fate for mine, if only I had not been so fond of you.

In the railway carriage I felt no desire to talk to my fellow passengers: I was carrying away great riches in my soul and there was no one with whom I could share them: they were all people who did not know you, who had not been that night at Leonidze's, who did not look for Kazbek in the dark and misty panorama from E. A. Bedia's terrace, poor unhappy wretches: they had no seats at those tables, for they only made an appearance in the world an hour before the departure of the train and for the sole purpose of filling up the reserved seats.

[1] An hotel in Tiflis.

[2] Boris Ivanovich Korneyev (1896–1958), journalist and translator, and his wife Serafima Vasilyevna.

[3] Nikolai Semyonovich Tikhonov, poet.

You can easily imagine, my dear friends, how many times I had occasion to live through again and again all that I had felt and seen. There was all the more time for it because we were late in arriving in Moscow by more than a day, in fact, by thirty hours. At first we were detained by a snowstorm for nine hours after leaving Baku, then we were stopped for a whole night behind Makhach-Kala by the derailment of a train at the next stage. Later we had been dropped out of the time-table, as we fully deserved: semaphores fell flat before us at the signal boxes and in the open country. Of course, it became clear to me that it was I and not the train that had dropped out of the timetable, for all my thoughts were not on the journey, but on the days I had spent with you.

Well, I have already talked so much nonsense that its quantity has, as it were, created a precedent for continuing in the same vein, but I must confess that on my arrival home I was confronted with a renewal of all that I had been through with Zina from the very beginning, with all its past dramatic intensity, but this time only the two of us under the peaceful and no longer disputed roof, so that at times I was overcome by doubt whether this stupid storm about a renewed aquaintance-ship was really necessary, considering that it had long been acknowledged and had become so obvious.

But now about something which is quite different from the sphere of pure stupidity, and is, indeed, a model of 'idiocy as such'.

On the basis of some telegrams in the English and Scandinavian press my father in a letter to me expresses his pleasure at my journey and . . . congratulates me (!). He had read, you see, that I was heading (!!) an expedition of writers which after-wards had crossed the Crimea in the *same train* (!!!) and my father very much liked the speech (!!!!) I had made in Tiflis (!!!!!).

My dear friends, is it worth living and working after that, when every one of us, without giving cause for it, suddenly becomes a victim of some goodness only knows what speculation, unreal not only in relation to us, but also from the point of view of its own interests, a speculation that does not even bother about where it should alight and lay its cuckoo's egg! At random and quite fortuitously (as, I suppose, are fields sown from aeroplanes), objects are chosen for some stock-jobbing deals and a man whose only desire is to live within the ardent confines of his own intense limitations becomes the hero of a stock exchange fairy-tale. . . .

Oh, Titian, how I'd have liked to know, but in all truth, who I am and what I am, so as to come to the judgement seat with my destiny in full possession of material evidence! Zina has an answer to this question. She thinks with all the personal interest of a great friend, that I am a good-for-nothing loafer and expresses doubts about our future life together if I do not at last sit down and do some work once more.

But she is not altogether right, because this tendency to form an attachment, of which I am only too conscious as the only definite thing about my character, is so powerful in me that it takes the place of work and seems to be my profession.

To become attached to places and to certain times of the day, to trees, to people, to the history of souls, which I need not be told, since the very reticence about it appears to me as heraldic figurative signs and so ready am I to tell their story for them—to become attached somehow not like a man, but stupidly, is the only thing that, though it may give no pleasure to anyone, I know and can do.

Among the messages with which I am about to burden you is one which I am afraid I cannot fully express, so much has it become part of my experience and so real is it to me. Its essence is that I send my regards to the poet Leonidze and to his poetry with the same kind of warmth as to his wife, his future and his household. I can force myself to be even more explicit: I send regards to the spark of *childishness* which runs through his hands and his manuscripts and descends upon his children. I do not speak of that false, Raphaelesque and over sentiment-alised conception of childhood, which does not exist except on chocolate boxes, but of the simplicity and foolishness and defencelessness of a child, of its electro-conductivity; of child-hood's ability to build a world on a toy and to be killed in crossing a road; of the spectacle of a child in the midst of a great life which has in the meantime forged ahead and with which he copes in a child-like fashion, simply, foolishly, quickly and defencelessly. But this kind of message is so weighty that it is best not to give it.

I learn from Zaytsev that B. N.[1] is a little worse and that he is confined to his bed, but the state of his health does not give cause for anxiety. The sequel of *Borderland*, the second volume of his memoirs, has just been published. I shall be seeing him shortly. I gave him your regards through Zaytsev.

Please, kiss Nita for me. Goodbye and come and see us soon. I am waiting impatiently for Tikhonov and Pavlenko, to find out what happened later. In their accounts I shall again see everything and again be with you. Just as one comes back sunburnt from the south so I came back with a fleeting glow from everything that has been and is no more, or rather which should have been extinguished and forgotten, but, to quote Yashvili, which has become a poet's friendship with his favourite flower, and that does not pass away.

Titian, I kiss you.

Your

B. P.

[1] Boris Nikolayevich (Andrey Bely).

1934

To P. M. Folyan[1]

14 February 1934

Dear Comrade Folyan,

I was very glad to receive your letter and if I am a little apprehensive about your expectations, which seem to me to be somewhat premature, it is not by any means your fault, for I am quite sure that you know nothing of what is happening here.

Nowadays, only news of his death is received as evidence of a relative change in a person's life, and that, too, with a certain feeling of condescension towards the dead man, to the rest we turn a deaf ear, even if it is a friendly one.

The point is that some time ago I wrote to Nikolai Mitsishvili and, I believe, also to G. V. Bebutov[2] about the surprises that awaited me at home on my return from Tiflis, but it would

[1] P. M. Folyan was the editor-in-chief of the Transcaucasian publishing house which was issuing an anthology *The Poets of Georgia* for the First All-Soviet Congress of Writers in the translations of Pasternak and Tikhonov and Vazha Pshavela's *Zmeyeyed* in Pasternak's translation.

[2] G. V. Bebutov, a Soviet literary scholar, who later edited the last edition of Pasternak's *Poems about Georgia* and *Georgian Poets*, published in Tiflis in 1958.

53

seem that it has remained a secret with the addressees. The children had measles, scarlet fever and chicken-pox, the boys were separated and sent to hospital, our flat was disinfected, etc., etc. When at the beginning of January there was a temporary break I took up several interlinear translations all at once, which, incidentally, I had only just then received from Goltsev.

When Andrey Bely died, I could not possibly refuse to take an active part in the planning of his funeral, the settlement of his immediate affairs, etc. This, besides, was quite in accordance with my feelings. At the end of January the Congress Organisation Committee received a telegram announcing the departure of a group of Georgian writers. Again there was a period of waiting and, I regret to say, the whole thing proved to be a false alarm (they did not arrive). At the same time the two-storeyed house in which I live was about to collapse as a result of the building of a tunnel for the Moscow Underground Railway. At first I was deprived of sleep because of my admiration for the work of the young people who day and night were producing miracles of gradual transformation of our familiar courtyard into something between German Essen and Greek Tartarus. But these miracles palled on me when my back staircase was blocked up, the stairs leading to the attic caved in and the back of my flat was turned into the only practicable highway for the rest of my neighbours who had found themselves in a much worse situation than I. For, anticipating the collapse of the walls, I was entitled to demand a new flat for myself with some hope of obtaining it some time or other. If my neighbours attempted to put in such a claim they would merely have enriched our folklore with more disinterested examples of creative art that produce no practical results whatsoever. It was while I was engaged in these efforts to obtain a flat, which were by no means hopeless, but which were not particularly helpful in advancing my work on Vazha Pshavela's poem, that, to my great delight, the families of Tabidze and Mitsishvili arrived (T. T. is down with influenza and will get up only tomorrow). Finally, my wife fell ill the other day with, it seems to us (the doctor has not yet diagnosed her illness), pneumonia.

I have written all this at such length to prove to you that if, unlike those who are ill or are just idle, someone in our republics does do some work against all reason and in spite of the elements, it is 1) the workers on the Metro, 2) myself and 3) Gaprindashvili.

All his interlinear translations are quite remarkable and, besides, he, too, happens to be a quite remarkable poet. To my regret, I have no time to write to him personally. I should also have liked to write to B. I. Korneyev. But these letters would take up too much of my time. I am compelled to write about my business and my private affairs in the same letters. Sometimes I write them in the hope that the second part will not remain the property only of those who receive them, but will go further afield with a wave of regards and commissions, in accordance with the instructions contained in them. But the truth is that everyone is so busy that I cannot possibly bear any grudge against Mitsishvili, whose head is in a whirl from the thousands of contradictory commissions he has been entrusted with. Everything that had been revised was sent on to him, but because of his lack of time my manuscripts find themselves in the position of pornographic postcards which are not shown to anyone. I have translated two poems by Chikovani and Abashidze.[1] If they had wanted to use them in *On the Border*, they could have done so, but I do not know whether B. I. or G. V. knows about it.

I should have liked very much to be able to tell you in answer

[1] Pasternak translated I. Abashidze's *Ballad of Salvation*.

to your impatient enquiry that I have not yet begun the translation of Vazha's poem, but to my great regret I have spoilt my
own pleasure because, apart from several poems by Nadiradze,
Grishashvili, Gaprindashvili and Mitsishvili (not counting the
above mentioned Chikovani and Abashidze), I have, in
addition, translated between two and three hundred lines of
Vazha's *Zmeyeyed*.

However, do not draw any rash conclusions from this. It
does not at all mean that tomorrow there will be three hundred
and fifty lines and the day after tomorrow four hundred. This
might have been the case if you had sent to my house a squad of
Tiflis militia men to cut off my telephone, to put a sentry
outside the door of my room, to go out to fetch milk for the
children, etc., etc. You would have liked the translations of
Vazha's poem to be published before the Congress [of the
Union of Soviet Writers] but the editors of our modern
anthologies, full of the same praiseworthy desires, advise me
to put off the publication for the time being because of the same
Congress and for the sake of the moderns. But neither you nor
they seem to take into consideration the fact that all sorts of
forms of life are mobilising themselves with no less zeal to take
part in the congress and most of all the microbes and bacteria
who have made up their minds to put an end to me and kill off
all my nearest and dearest on the very eve of the congress
and most certainly not after.

I am working on the translations all at once, I do not go out
for walks, I do not read books, I have not seen my son for the
last two months, although he lives only within a twenty
minutes' bus ride from me—what more can I do for you and
Gudiashvili to whom I send my warmest regards and whose
consent to illustrate the book I welcome as the first good news
I've had throughout these nine pages. I cannot tell you anything more. I press your hand warmly. Gaprindashvili is a fine

fellow and I like him so much that I really am afraid that he may have been having as much fun during these two and a half stormy months as I have.

Give my cordial regards to our mutual friends. Goodbye.

With true respect,

B. Pasternak

Do me the favour of conveying even part of what I have told you to the few people I love and whose friendship I greatly value. I am very sorry I cannot write to them personally.

To Titian and Nina Tabidze

8 December 1934[1]

My dear Nina Alexandrovna and Titian,

Oh, both of you are so dear to me! But then we shall still find more and more in life that we have in common and we shall still live so intensely one by the other, shan't we? So why write letters to one another?

All I want at the moment is to free myself from my servitude, from my prose. It would take too long to tell you why I go on writing it.

When I address you as my nearest and dearest, my equals, as people whom I can understand emotionally—those are not empty, idle words. When you come, ask Klavdiya Nikolaevna.[2]

In my unposted letters I wrote to you about myself. That I feel somewhat like a bottle of hard glue in which the best of what I have experienced in life is stuck together in one lump.

[1] This is the postmark date.
[2] Andrey Bely's wife.

I enumerated in them the things which bound me to you: Roland, my eldest sister, the present revolutionary Germany which suddenly appeared as the natural continuation of Rilke, and so on. Then I suddenly remembered that you, Nina, ought surely to know about these things when next door to you you have such a living bottle as Titian. And, say what you like, Titian is one of the most powerful lyrical poets of all of them. I knew it even before I knew him. But he is too near to me. Just as about myself, I dare not acknowledge it even to myself. Sometimes I completely sacrificed him just as I did myself. Can you understand it? But did you hear what happened in the conference hall when I walked over to him? To your little dogs,[1] Nina. Titian will be the heart of the Moscow book. He will save it.

But enough, enough! This letter will not be posted either.

When I saw *Zmeyeyed* in book form my heart contracted from the *impossibility* of saying to whom I owed it. I should have said it to Euphemia Alexandrovna.

During the first month after my return I remembered so clearly every place in Tiflis and every moment I spent there and it is this that did the work for me and she was the person who brought it all back to me.

It is not necessary to tell her because she knows it without our telling her. Only she knows it as everyone, including Zina, knows it: without ever understanding anything.

To understand a completely different world, a completely different style and way of life—that is not a question of places or moments or even of Tiflis, or even perhaps of the earth: it is an admission by chance to a close participation in the affairs of history and in its future, it is a boundless, never-ending love story of a few specially favoured people, beneath a sky that covers them with the meaning of one common date. It is

[1] A reference to Tabidze's poem *Village Night*, translated by Pasternak.

the glue I have mentioned before, it is you and I, it is our joined hands.

I am sending you my summer photograph. It was taken by an ordinary Odoevsky schoolmaster. I did not feel embarrassed in his presence and that is why it came out so well.

I embrace you, Titian.

Your

B.

1935

To Titian Tabidze

10 March 1935. Evening

Dear Titian,

I woke up at eight this morning. Zina says that 'if I were you, I'd have seen Titian off'. It was my intention to do that. Shortly after nine, still unwashed and undressed, I rang up Zhango to find out exactly at what time and from what station your train was leaving. He said at half past ten. I had still to wash and do all the usual things one does do in the morning. I reconciled myself easily to the idea that I was too late to see you off: 1) you did not want it; 2) you were still here with me in spirit, your departure had not yet taken place, it was still easy to reconcile oneself to the facts.

What happened later was rather silly. During the whole of the past year I cannot remember a more melancholy and more futile day. I sat down to do some work. I could not do a thing, everything seemed to go wrong. For no reason at all I was overcome by a fit of melancholy which made me feel drowsy and I think I must have fallen asleep at my desk. I then lay down, lay about for an hour without falling asleep. Then I

60

went off to town on some business. I met Paolo in the street. He said that the train had left at half past eleven. So I could have just managed to see you on that wonderfully fresh morning! This piece of news did not improve my spirits. I then went to see Yevgeniya Vladimirovna.[1] She is cross with me, and we had rather a sad talk. Next I walked along Tversky Boulevard—looked at my watch: it was still two o'clock, the dull Northern before-dinner-time, and in melancholy [next page is missing]. . . .

I shall find it difficult without you. It will take me a long time to get used to your absence.

Goodbye, my dear.

Kiss Nina and Nita. I know that you will be thinking of me sometimes: do not force yourself to write to me. I know how difficult we writers find it. I embrace you.

Your
B.

To Titian Tabidze

6 October 1935

My golden Tabidze,

It would take a long time to tell you what has been happening to me all this summer. I am still far from well, but I have made up my mind to pay no attention to my heart, my liver, my sleep, or my nerves. The main thing is that I am home again with Zina and can recognise myself a little, not, it is true, as I was before, but still as if I were the same person. One day I shall tell you in detail what I have been through during

---

[1] Yevgeniya Vladimirovna Muratova, Pasternak's first wife.

those four months, but for the time being I shall confine myself to what you, and only you, ought to know.

During those agonising days of suffering I did not stop loving my dear ones and my old friends, I did not forget Paolo and Heinrich Gustavovich,[1] I did not turn away from my best friends. In Paris I met Marina Ts.[2] But during this journey, as during the numerous and aimless absences in different rest houses where I spent my convalescence and where I went out of my mind from worry and loneliness, I invariably took with me as talismans: constant thoughts of Z. N., one letter by Rainer Maria Rilke, and one of yours, written in the spring— remember? I often put it under my pillow at night in a kind of superstitious hope that it might bring me sleep, from the lack of which I suffered so much all summer.

I told Shcherbakov,[3] with whom I shared a cabin from London to Leningrad, a lot about you. It was the worst time of my trials, a kind of sickness of the soul, a sensation of the end without any visible approach of death, a most unimaginable state of depression. Every time I fell to thinking about what was going to happen next, I imagined that I would ask Nina to let me have you and idle away the rest of the day with you, Titian, somewhere near the Kazbek. But those were meditations based on several blackest assumptions.

All this is over now. I am saddened and at times frightened by the abrupt change that has taken place in me this year. But I do not want to have any more medical treatment or to go anywhere to rest or to convalesce. I want to try to do some work (for over four months I did nothing).

Need I say how grateful I am to you for remembering me,

[1] H. G. Neuhaus, a distinguished Soviet pianist and musicologist.
[2] The poet Marina Tsvetaeva.
[3] Alexander Sergeyevich Shcherbakov (1901–45), at the time Secretary of the Union of Soviet Writers.

for the warmth and generosity of your heart. You know how much I love you—I love only Zina more than you. My warmest regards to dearest Nina and Nitochka.

Your
B.

I'll write to you again. I have only just arrived in town, unpacked my things and found your new letter, and these few words of mine are instead of a telegram. Warm and cordial regards to Paolo. That friendship, too, is immutable—in it, too, there is great happiness.

1936

To Titian and Nina Tabidze

8 April 1936

My dear friends Titian and Nina,

For over a week I have been carrying about in my pocket a most tender telegram to both of you. But I am ashamed to hand it in at the post office, where the clerks on duty have no time for heartfelt effusions or for telegrams in that style. I have been intending all the time to change it for a more business-like and less warm one. Finally, after a long time, I gave up that idea, too.

What is keeping you, Titian? Why are you not coming? I did not want to telegraph you about my love and loyalty. You know that already and must have been bored with it for a long time. I wanted to tell you not to lose heart, to believe in yourself and stand firm in spite of temporary misunderstandings. I was so delighted by your telephone call! Even Nina came to the phone—thank you! But it was difficult to talk. You did not hear me, but I heard you excellently.

There is a great deal that is deceptive and indefinite in the painful discords of the recent past. I felt it at once.[1]

[1] A reference to the articles published in connection with the debate about formalism in 1936.

64

If there is a particle of truth in anything that has been published and discussed, it is only that it coincides with the overall
plan of the times, with its historic infinity. But how can infinity be a particle, and of such a worthless whole as the critical
semolina porridge which people have been so touchingly
gulping down for over a month? Here is the answer: this
truth was ladled out in a dismally weak solution. . . .

Don't believe in solutions, Titian! Believe precisely in that
line, precisely out of loyalty to the revolution believe rather in
yourself, Titian Tabidze, for, say what you like, the chemistry
of your way of thinking dissolves everything in the world,
whatever you may call it, at a higher temperature than is
acceptable to the 'Literaries' or the 'Evenings'.[1] And even if
you did not want it, the revolution has been dissolved by us
more strongly and more strikingly than you could decant
it from a debating tap. Do not turn to public charity, my
friend. Rely only on yourself. Dig more deeply with your
drill without fear or favour, but inside yourself, inside yourself. If you do not find the people, the earth and the heaven
there, then give up your search, for then there is nowhere
else to search. That would be clear even if we did not know
anyone searching in a different way. Are there so few of them?
The fruits of their labours are here for all to see.

You need not worry. I am not the only one who appreciates
you and believes in you. Don't believe in solutions. Believe in
revolution as a whole, believe in the future, the new promptings of your heart, the spectacle of life, and not the construction
put on things by the Union of Soviet Writers, which will be
changed all of a sudden before you have had time to sneeze—
believe in the Age and not in the week of the formalist.

I have been feeling on top of the world all this month. Only

[1] A veiled reference to *The Literary Gazette*, the official organ of the
Union of Soviet Writers, and the evening *Izvestia*.

once have I had an attack of flu, which lasted three days. I was terribly glad to see Paolo. But he is such a child and it is very difficult to argue with him. The moment he begins talking awful drivel and his arguments have to be disputed, he becomes the spitting image of Medea (an extraordinary likeness!) and you feel so touched that you lose heart.

Come as soon as possible. I have rarely been as composed as I am now. I have not changed a bit. It was only in the idiotic verses written before Minsk and which will be published soon in *Znamya* that I removed the dedication to Leonidze for fear that he might get into trouble because of a certain independence of its content.

But some kind of period in general literary life and in my own personally has come to an end. Mine came to an end even earlier: I could not cope with my prose, I fell sick mentally, I did translations. Do I know what I must do next? I do. Only I won't tell it to anyone, perhaps only to you, and that, too, under a seal of great secrecy. But in a completely different line from the nonsense in *Znamya*. There it is only a blank explosion, an unsubstantiated emptiness, an outlet to perplexity.

But I shall work, let us say, from the beginning of autumn, if I am alive and well.

Regards to everybody. Kiss Nina and Nita affectionately. I embrace you with all my heart. Forgive the silly tone of this letter. The reason: my tooth is aching savagely, but my heart is gay and makes me do all sorts of silly things. Do come!

Your

B.

To Titian and Nina Tabidze

1 October 1936

My dear Titian and Nina,

You are spoiling us again. I am writing from Peredelkino (we shall probably spend the winter here). I am writing without having seen Sofia Andreyevna.[1] What abundance has come tumbling down on us from you again! A whole orchard with wine for two age groups: children and grown-ups. How are we to thank you for it all!

And—I surmise—before you had had time to pack the basket and take it to the railway station to give to dear and incomparable S. A., Vitya Goltsev appeared with the words: 'Look, what prattling dull nonsense your Borya has perpetrated!'

No, seriously. Have you ever seen anything like it? Zina as well as Yevgeny Vladimirovich just shook their heads and refused to believe that I would allow it to be published.

Nina, Nina, Titian, my precious one, what can be happening to me, my dear friends? Where do I get this verbiage and boredom, this soullessness and stupidity from? Am I the only one guilty of it? All I can say in self-justification is that I kept refusing, I knew that until I was successful in mastering the prose that would set me free and leave me to my own devices, I ought not to think of writing any poetry for a long, long time, for now my mind is not set on poetry, but is far, far away from it. But what can I do? I explained it to Victor, and he is no fool and a friend of mine, but it was just like talking to a blank wall!

Do not try to comfort me, let me comfort you instead. Don't think for a moment, Titian and Nina, that I am really

---

[1] S. A. Tolstoy, Leo Tolstoy's granddaughter, wife of S. A. Esenin.

finished, that everything I write will be of the same kind now. You will see, I will write my prose. I began writing it again a few days ago. One thing I do know: it will be alive. It is here, indeed, that those traces of life will be found which I seemed to have lost since *The Second Birth*.

Yes, but how could one have written such a silly three-foot poem, such a bird-like, such fatuous twit-twit-twit about Georgia? What an abomination to say so little about Paolo![1] Are you still as friendly with him as you used to be? Oh, I wish you were! After sending off that rhymed disgrace I kept thinking of him for nights on end. I remembered his breadth of vision, the nobility of his attitudes towards me during the most crucial moments of my soul. What an irreproachable insight of a great man with a large heart and a wide mental outlook! Will he forgive me the levity of these lines about him (there is nothing bad in them, but was it like that that one should have spoken about him?), will he forgive my carping criticisms of him this year? Oh, from what petty positions I judged him! I do not regret the 'positions': more generally accepted ones are no bigger. But how did I dare to measure him with such a petty yardstick? I have not changed, I know: revolution is not in that ridiculous *Literary Gazette*, nor in literary organisations, nor in competitions in timidity, but in its sweeping outlines and its central personalities. For the time being it can be discerned only in the greatest. That is why it is so difficult: it will come to life when it will be seen in the smallest. And, of course, it will be.

I have not changed, I say, but I suddenly remembered Paolo as he truly was and I could not understand what happened to me in winter, and who gave me the right to look for changes in him and ascribe them to him without any foundation. I was

[1] A reference to the cycle *Travel Notes* (summer, 1936). The poem *For the Threshold of the Past* was dedicated to Paolo Yashvili.

blinded at the time by that devilish debate. It was while in this cultural-enlightened trance that I suddenly *forgot that I loved him*.

And you, Titian? I can imagine what you must have felt when you read about the waterfall, etc.[1] And that at a moment when the publication of your book has brought a fresh breath of air into our literature, has reminded us of poetry, of the time when there were such people as poets, and, however improbable this may sound, that one of them has survived, one in the whole Soviet Union. On my word of honour, it is in such a spirit that one shares this joy.

                                         9 October 1936
This letter has been lying here for some time and I do not know why I am not posting it. I was in town, rang up S. A., but she was not at home. I wanted to ask her to convey our thanks to you. Do not attach any particular importance to the drivel in this letter. We have had many more excitements since then,[2] and one thing counterbalances the other. I kiss the two of you and Nita affectionately.

                                         Your
                                         B.

[1] A reference to a poem of the cycle *The Unceasing Lapping of the Fields*.
[2] A reference to the purges.

1937

To T. G. Yashvili

28 August 1937

My dear, poor Tamara Georgiyevna,

What's all this? For a month I lived as though nothing had been happening and I knew nothing. I have known about it for about two weeks, and all the time I go on writing to you, writing and tearing it up. My existence no longer has any value, I am myself in need of comforting and I do no know what to say to you that would not strike you as idealistic verbiage and highfalutin pharisaism.

When I was told about it the first time, I did not believe it. It was confirmed to me in town on the seventeenth. The shades and half-shades fell away. The news gripped me by the throat, I was in its power and still am. Not everything that I experienced under the impact of that terrible fact is irremediable and death-dealing—not everything.

When again and again I come to the realisation that never again shall I see that wonderful face with its high, inspired forehead and laughing eyes and never hear the voice whose very sound was fascinating from its overflow of ideas, I burst into tears, I toss about in anguish and can find no place for myself. With thousands of well-remembered details my memory shows him to me in all the changes of the situations we have been through together: in the streets of several towns, at excursions to the sea and the mountains, at your home and at my home, on our latest journeys, when presiding at conferences and on rostrums. The memory wounds and drives the pain of bereavement to a point of insanity, flies in my face with reproach: what have I done to be punished by an eternity of this parting?

But it happened on the very first day, the 17th, that its irreversibility cleansed me and brought me down to elementary facts which cannot be disputed, as in childhood, when after crying yourself into a state of torpor you suddenly want to eat and sleep from sheer fatigue. That blow was so powerful that it flung me far away from everything urban, from everything that is loud, not by right, not from necessity complicated, hysterically indifferent, eloquently empty. 'What nonsense,' I said to myself again and again, 'Paolo? The Paolo I knew so well that I did not even care to analyse how I loved him, Paolo—the name of my delight, and everything that an average man A. or an average man B. might communicate to me with a serious air, men who will be forgotten in a moment. This,' I thought, 'is for the future.' Everyone has to die anyway, and, moreover, in some kind of definite surroundings. So they will say: this life, preserved by posterity, came to an end in the summer of 1937, and they will add the authentic facts of the time in question: the topics that occupied the minds of the public, the names of the papers, the names of acquaintances. In exactly the same way as in reference to some other age one would talk of wigs and jabots or, further back in time, of hunts with falcons.

So I carried this from town and got off at our station of

Peredelkino. I knew that when I opened my mouth on the veranda to tell this to Zina, my voice would break and everything would be repeated afresh. But for the time being, on the way home, I gave myself up more and more, without relapsing, to the purifying force of grief, and how far did it take me!

I would have liked to have a bathe. The day was drawing to a close. On the bank, in the shady ravine, when, after lying down comfortably, I gradually recovered from the agitations of my journey, I suddenly began to catch, here and there, the features of some kind of marvellous likeness to the deceased. It was all inexpressibly wonderful and terribly reminiscent of him. I saw bits and pieces of his spirit and style: his grass and water, his autumnal, setting sun, his stillness, rawness and secretiveness. So, indeed, might he have said, how they were burning and hiding, winking at each other and dying out. The sunset seemed to imitate him or reproduce him in memory.

I began thinking of him somehow in a new way. I always admired his talent, his unsurpassable flair for the picturesque, rare not only in Georgian literature, not only in the whole of our modern literature, but precious at any and every time. He always astonished me. People have letters which show how highly I thought of him. But it was for the first time that I began thinking of him quite apart from what I felt for him. Just as one moves away from something very, very big, his absolute outlines began to take shape only at the fateful distance of his loss: what he was away from us, away from me, Titian and Gogla, what he was not only apart from our admiration of him and our desire to see him victorious, but, on the contrary, in defiance of our love: what he was himself with the water and the woods, and God and the future.

Need I expatiate on that? About him who in the future will be the Georgian Mayakovsky, or whose models the future young literature, if it is destined to develop, will emulate and study. But that side of immortality never troubled me. What surprises me is something else, however difficult it may be to express it: how much of him there remains in what he touched and what he named: in the hours of the day, in the flowers and animals, in the verdure of the woods, in the autumn sky. We lived and did not know the power he wielded among us, the authority that he still retains.

Dear Tamara Georgiyevna, forgive me. One must not write like that, one must not—to you. Poetry, and bad poetry at that, is out of place here. But I'll send off what I've written all the same, or when else shall I at last say the only thing that matters, that draws me so powerfully to you and to the unimaginably precious Medea? That is not complicated, and you know it without me. Though you have no lack of friends and never will have, number me among them. However difficult my existence has become of late, nothing will be impossible for me so far as you are concerned. How much I should have liked to see you! I am asking Titian and Nina to embrace you for me, to be together with you and weep with you. And once more forgive me for this silly, feeble letter. But, then, I know nothing, nothing, even now. Would you write to me, some time afterwards, when you feel able to do so?

All yours,

B. P.

Forgive me once more. In your grief, what does the extent of mine matter to you or, what is even more tactless, the details describing how I was walking home and what I had been thinking at the time?

1938

To Nina Tabidze

Do you realise, Nina, how much I miss you? Separation from you, from Nita, from your atmosphere, from the conversation we might have had together, if only we could have met, can be compared only with my longing for my sisters and my parents whom I have not seen for fifteen years.

I always thought that I loved Titian, but what I did not know was the place in my life that, unconsciously and in spite of myself, belongs to him. I regarded it as a feeling. I did not realise that it was a magical fact.

How many times did we feast, swear oaths of loyalty (our poor P.[1] was, of course, also present: you don't think I shall ever forget him, do you?), show off, exaggerate! How many reasons were there for always being afraid that the magical *nothing* might become a fact. And suddenly how much more intimate and more fervent it turned out to be!

How feeble was the name given to it all! How extraordinary is the *real* force of that relentless, absorbing, insane bond!

I often dream of you, sometimes of you and sometimes of us all, of the places we have been together with the intricate

[1] Paolo Yashvili.

intermingling with the members of my family. Last winter when it was all connected *only* with horror and suffering, I sometimes woke up in tears, thinking that what pained me was not my own pain, but that I had become a part of your own terrible shock and a part of yourself, and that was why it was so intense. I find this madness hard to explain.

But now, thank God, it is over. I am not asking you to tell me anything. Though knowing much less than you, I still know enough to live in hope. I know that, according to some higher plan, our new, poignant, temporarily postponed re-union has been predetermined in all its details, and it is our task not to spoil the meeting, that is to say, to live long enough to be there. I could write to you endlessly about it, but it's no use.

I find things a little more difficult. But it is my own fault. I was never very good at enthusiasm. During the last two years it became more than I could bear—that is understandable.

On the eve of 1938 I became the father of a boy. Zina gave birth to him exactly at midnight to the clinking of glasses in our dining-room.

I wanted to call him Paul[1] (I cannot get that life out of my mind and heart: is there any need for me to assure you of that?), but Zina burst into tears, so much was she frightened at this close connection with the image of grief and bitterness and mysterious ending, and, falling back on the nearest relation, I called him Leonid after my father.

Vitya[2] will tell you the rest. All honour and glory to his heart for volunteering to see you. You can tell him that.

I am haunted by a dream: I am about to sign a big contract, I am getting an advance, I fly to you for a day, I spend it with you, listen to your stories all day long, tell you something in

[1] After Paolo Yashvili.
[2] V. V. Goltsev.

75

return, and go back the same day. But nobody signs big contracts with me. Still? What about you? I don't know what is beneficial or harmful to you in your situation, what can or cannot be done.

If only fate would bring you and Nita to us at 17–19, Lavrushinsky Lane, flat 72! How happy I would be if you were to write to me about it.

I kiss your hands.

If you see Tamara Georgiyevna, tell her all this.

Your
Borya

1939

To G. N. and E. A. Leonidze

12 January 1939

Dear Gogla[1] and Euphemia Alexandrovna,

I was deeply touched by your good wishes—thank you. I did not reply at once, as any decent man would have done, because I was ill in bed and alone in the apartment. Now I am well again and, amidst the noise of the children who have just returned from their holidays, I am replying, making up for the omission. What am I to tell you?

My impression of your house and your domestic life has, somehow, always been of something out of a fairy-tale, something exhilarating. You know that. I was again excited when from this union of strength, beauty and happiness I was sent your best wishes for the New Year. What shall I wish you? That it shall always be like that and that you should never know old age. That your word and your two names should be sufficient to conjure up again the hill leading to Sololaki[2] on a winter evening, with the trees and buildings of pronouncedly

[1] Georgy Leonidze's nickname.
[2] A suburb of Tiflis where Leonidze lived

European architecture, which arouses in one's heart a sense of unrest as it does in Petersburg, not the unrest of admiration or enthusiasm, but the unrest of a half-guessed plot of a story: here somewhere, in one of the windows (what has the street to do with it, why the trees?), a young name bursts in, intrudes into history and stays in it: this is more than just a poet, more than even a good one, it is a personality who himself impinges on one's imagination as though he were the hero of a fairy-tale.

I'm afraid I am getting old, that is to say, I am feeling more often and more strongly the scantiness of the years and the powers that are left to me. I am ashamed to remember the reception we gave to you and Chikovani that time in Peredelkino. But apart from mentioning the fact that with the years and in general I seem to live more and more in an attic, it was a time of quite unbearable shame and grief, I felt ashamed that we went on moving about, talking and smiling.

I am told you are planning to come here at the end of January. That would be nice!

I embrace you, Gogla, and kiss the hand of Euphemia Alexandrovna. I wish you health and happiness, and may the Lord guard your little girls.

Your

B. Pasternak

P.S. I'm sorry to have written such terrible stupidities to you. It isn't intentionally, of course, that is, I was thinking that it would turn out to be more intelligent. This is because whenever I think of you I let my imagination run away with me: that is how I see you.

1939–40

To Nina Tabidze

Dear Nina,

Forgive me for writing to you. I am sure I ought not to worry you. Recently, quite recently I heard a rumour that Titian was dead. You can imagine what I felt. But a few hours ago I was told that the surmise was false and that there are proofs to the contrary. I returned home reeling with joy and, while writing to you, this belief is transformed into a certainty. But, please, confirm it. Tell me that he is alive. Wire or write to me.

Nina, Nina, this is what I want from you: that whatever heaven may send us you should know that all of me and all my life and reason belong to you and Nita and are at your service. During the three unhappy days that I tried to believe the terrible rumour, I realised that it would be for me not only a boundless grief, but also such a change in my whole life that after it not one of its joys would be dear to me, for I should have no one to share it with. I loved the thought that I lived for him and he for me, and if anything had happened, the future would have lost all meaning for me. Nina, I don't know what I am writing to you. But I do not give up hope.

Your Borya

79

1940

To Nina Tabidze

24 November 1940

Forgive me, dear Nina, for not having written to you for so
long. I began writing a letter to you on the fourteenth, but I
will start a new one. But, apart from that, I must apologise for
not having thanked you at once for your last letter. I have told
you my reasons on a postcard: I did not know for a long time
about the arrival of the Andronikovs[1] and that they had a letter
for me from you.

Now about the letter. I am grieved, Nina, that you work
yourself up and torment yourself for wrong reasons. Why do
you tear up the letters to me, write them several times, set
yourself some kind of aim, are not satisfied with some kind of
expression? There are no people around me with whom I
feel so near and simple as with you. Harsh things have bound
me to you: grief and pride.

Simon and Marika have been here for a long time. We met a
few times. They have, each of them, their own good qualities, I
am fond of both of them, and if they wished, they could, with

---

[1] I. L. Andronikov and his wife V. A. Andronikov.

their intelligence and powers of observation, tell you a great deal about Zina and myself, about our literary life, about life in general, and so on and so forth. He gave a party here which was a great success. Tell them that I wrote to you about it—they will like that and they will have deserved it of you.

I shall purposely ask them not to convey anything from me to you, except my regards, so as not to influence their stories. Both of them know very well that Titian and you are dearer to me than anyone else in the world.

I feel an irresistible urge to leave with them and Vitya in order to see you. But I am afraid to leave. I gave *Hamlet* to the theatre (it will be performed by the Moscow Art Theatre) and I may be needed by them at any moment. All the more so as you will be coming to visit us, won't you?

Forgive the inkstains on my letter: we've been paying so many visits during the last few nights that I can hardly control my hand (this is something more for you when you see Chikovani). Tell him that I wrote to you after meeting him at Goltsev's and that he, Simon, is 'now in fashion and—the hit of our season'. Dear Nina, I wish I could amuse you by something or tell you something cheerful, but I have a headache and I'm afraid it wouldn't come off. Do come, please: there are so many things I'd like to tell you and say to you.

Goodbye, my dear friend. I kiss you. It seems to me as if I had never taken leave of Titian and yourself and I must restrain myself so that my letters to you should not appear to be love letters and make people laugh. Goodbye, dear friend.

P.S. When Ch. and Vitya[1] start telling you about me, assume a proud look and say: 'I know everything. He writes to me every day.' Kiss Nita. I'd gladly give part of my life to make your life happier. I worship you.

Your B. P.

[1] S. I. Chikovani and V. V. Goltsev.

To Nina Tabidze

27 December 1940

Nina, a happy New Year! I love you very much and if you find no traces of it in my letters, it means that they were written by fatigue, despair and haste. I am very sorry to have written to you the other day in a hurry and at odd moments.

I have just returned from town and am falling asleep with fatigue while writing this letter, though at the same time you are all the time before my eyes. Nina, you are a person of such *importance* in my life that sometimes I have a feeling that I love Zina because you have given me permission to love her.

Gradually things are getting more settled in town. I expect I shall still be the object of all sorts of attacks, but fundamentally the attitude towards me is wonderful and, generally, I am, of course, a terribly happy man.

I am writing this to you, because I know that I shall some day share this happiness with you and with T.,[1] that somehow or other the four of us together with some friends will some day dine on all that we have lived through, tastefully, beautifully, all through a summer night or several nights, and will stay at each other's homes, feeling so happy, so languid, so reposeful!

Titian is alive and is somewhere not very far away and there is less and less time to wait. T. is a person essential to my existence, he is the god of my life, in the Greek and mythological sense. I can't help thinking that I could not have been so happy, that I could not have loved you, or have occupied such a place in time and expected so much for myself in the future, if T. had not been part of it.

Forgive me, darling Nina, for letting my imagination run

[1] Titian Tabidze.

away with me so freely and for trying to interfere with so difficult, sacred and intimate a thing as our non-fictional life. On my word of honour, it is not thoughtlessness and I write through tears.

So, please, add also my warm breath to the warmth you and your friends have breathed on New Year's Eve. Let that be truly a meeting.

Your most devoted to you and Nita and to all yours

B. P.

P.S. Things will be better in 1941, you'll see.

1941

To T. T. Tabidze

6 February 1941

Dear Nita,

I dearly wish I could see you. I don't suppose I should have recognised you at all. From one of your mother's letters I concluded, mistakenly perhaps, and if so, please, forgive me, that the uncertainty of the future and the monotony of the present sometimes undermine your strength by their all too apparent emptiness. I know about these things from my elder son, so, please, don't be angry with me for having decided to write to you.

Nita, you were separated from your father by force, and from *such* a father, and yet you grew up and did not go under. Morally, you are almost a heroine, you are part of heroic history and the product of heroism. You are the last person to give in to depression.

All your deprivations will be compensated a hundredfold. The main thing is that we all believe that your greatest joy in future will be your meeting with your father, his return. Is it worthwhile, is it necessary to say anything else?

At any rate, I want you to know this. It is only the hope to see part of your dazzling future—vital, many-sided, abounding in all sorts of events, morally justified and boundless so far as spiritual values are concerned—that makes us, worn out and old as we are, hang on to life and desire and value it in any of its forms. However far it may be, everything that is far will one day be near.

Your

B. P.

To Nina Tabidze

21 March 1941

. . . You must be surprised that I never said a single word about Gaprindashvili's death. Nevertheless, it is not unintentionally. My ideas about him are very close to my ideas about myself, though he, poor fellow, is no longer with us, while I am still alive and carrying on with my endeavours to put the final touch to my scandalous position. Though we may not be alike, there is in both our cases the same spiritual compactness, the same depth of eye, the same ability and desire to take down everything around us in images, and, finally, the same futility and inopportuneness of a wasted life.

Nina, I have a request to make to you. Last summer I had a visit from the actors of your Russian theatre in Tiflis. They took the text of my *Hamlet* for a production of the play. Could you perhaps find out indirectly why it did not come off (otherwise I should have heard how their work was proceeding).

Write to me about it as soon as you have found out, without sparing me.

It's a funny kind of letter, Nina, isn't it? Think before you answer it. Do not write all sorts of reassuring trifles to me, but if you have some ideas about this, share them with me. I kiss you.

Your
Borya

To Nina Tabidze

9 May 1941

Dear Nina,

Thank you very much for your new letter and Gaprindash-vili's widow for the sonnet, which has given me great joy. Has she a copy of it? If not, I'll copy it and, if she wants it, return the original, which I should very much have liked to keep all the same. To be quite frank about it, the beginning of the sonnet is wonderful, but the other parts bear the stamp of the rhythmic conventionality peculiar to this form of verse, which even Balmont could do nothing about. And so, once more: convey my sincere condolences and deep gratitude to her.

Dear Nina, you saw the two Leonidzes. This is how it happened. I did not know at all that Euphemia Alexandrovna was in Moscow. As for Gogla, I thought that he was going to stay for a long time. I had some rush job and during the last few days I worked at it even at night. When I finished it, I left in the evening for Moscow. As it happened, they were leaving next day and were giving a farewell banquet at twelve o'clock at night at the 'Aragva'. It was there that we met. It was a very very long time since I had met them without the slightest embarrassment, with such a joyful and cordial feeling. The dinner, I'm sure, must have cost them at least several thousand roubles, but I'm no less sure that they were terribly bored. I felt absolutely at home and behaved like a terrible lout, saying everything that entered my head. . . . I got on extremely well with Gogla and he was very simple and natural. I felt so happy for the following reason: I am again in the same mood as last autumn, I shall certainly write my own poetry, and I am already working at it. Some kind of subtle aspects (in regard to art and life) have come to life in me. You came too late to see them: I was like that before my first marriage. Give my regards to both Leonidzes. I should like to see them very, very much, and I know that we shall soon meet again.

What poems did you have in mind, Nina, when you asked me to send them to you? I have only published a volume of selected translations. I will send it to you. The only thing worth noticing there is the section *Small Adaptations*, the rest are very old works. (*The Prince of Homburg*, 1918, *Hans Sachs*, 1919, and, published in a separate volume, *The Broken Jug*, as early as 1914.)[1]

Nina, you simply must come and stay with us for a rest this year. When I mention your name, Lyonichka[2] at once asks: 'Which Nina—mine?', as distinct from Fedin's. He is used to it and calls you 'my Nina'. I'm enclosing his photograph. Show it to Nita and give her my regards. Have you recovered from your illness? I kiss you affectionately. Adik is not going to have an operation. He is getting very thin.

Your Borya

[1] *The Prince of Homburg* and *The Broken Jug* are works by the German poet and dramatist Heinrich von Kleist.
[2] Pasternak's son Leonid.

To G. N. Leonidze

20 May 1941

Dear Gogla,

How are Euphemia Alexandrovna's eyes and how is she in general?

I have been thinking a lot about you recently. Zina moved to our country cottage a short while ago and she brought your telegram from Rostov. The charming thought of sending it must have occurred to you at the very moment when I was writing to Nina and, I'm sure, I told her something about our meeting because, I remember, I was going to.

I wish you and your family the best of health with all my heart. I think you find the same sort of weather agrees with you, too. I wish you a summer like a book, so that one could relive the world again from its very beginning. You and I have many friends, people who are both charming and worthy, but there are hardly any artists among them.

I press your hand warmly,

Your
B. Pasternak

1942

To Nina Tabidze

20 March 1942

Dear Nina,

The resumption of our correspondence is equivalent to a return to Moscow or to a return safe and sound to all my life from one insignificant and approximate part of it. And now it will come to pass!

Where are you and how are you, where is Nita, is your mother still alive, have you heard anything about Titian? Do you know that Heinrich Gustavovich has found himself in the same position as in Moscow since December? Since the end of September Adik has been in his clinic in Nizhny Ufaley in the Urals. Chistopol is not on the railway and we have been cut off from him all the time. His condition is very bad. He has contracted tuberculosis of the spine. His leg is in such a condition that the possibility of its amputation cannot be excluded. But will this sacrifice—if it has to be made—save his life? Zina does not believe it. For her, for me, for anyone you can think of, Adik is an object of endless tears. Please, write to him. He will be delighted with your letter. A great many

89

friends write to him from here, from Moscow and from Tash-
kent. He is greatly changed. He has grown serious and thought-
ful and writes wonderful letters. Do not, of course, touch upon
the naked truth in all its starkness as I am telling it to you. But
he knows it in a less stark form.

Zina and I will go and see him in the spring. I shall also have
to go to Moscow. I do not know yet which of these journeys
will be first and which second. His address is: Nizhny Ufaley,
Chelyabinsky Region, Red Rose Clinic, to Andrian Neuhaus.

Zina has got a job with the Literary Fund as a nurse-
superintendent of the Children's Home, in which Lyonichka
is being brought up. Stasik,[1] too, is there, in the boarding
school for older children. Fedin and Leonov are also here with
me in Chistopol. Earlier, in the summer months, Aseyev and
Trenyov lived here. In the autumn Marina Tsvetaeva hanged
herself in the neighbouring town of Yelabug-on-the-Kama. If
she had held out for another month, Konstantin Alexandrovich
[Fedin] and I would have gone to see her and got her the same
subsistence as we have enjoyed ourselves. She would have
managed to find some work like us, she could have taken part
in the literary evenings we organised and could have lived in
Chistopol, where she had been refused a permit to settle and
where she was trying hard to escape to from godforsaken
Yelabug (incidentally, I lived there in 1915, all my Kamas and
Urals were quite near!). It will always remain an unsolved
mystery to me how her situation could have remained so
desperate and without relief next to, and with the knowledge
of, Trenyov and Aseyev, who are both laureates with literary
prizes and have public influence and who both had a high
opinion of her. She was a poet of great potentialities. I knew her
so well and loved her person and her work so much that,
though I was in Moscow and this happened here on the Kama

[1] S. G. Neuhaus, Zina Pasternak's son by her first marriage.

and though I knew nothing and had nothing to do with it, I am, for all that, the only one to blame for this bitter sin of omission.

Do you know that Afinogenov is dead? He and his wife worked in the Information Bureau and stayed in Moscow till the last moment and were then evacuated to Kuybyshev together with their office. Both of them with their children were to be sent to America for radio work. From Kuybyshev Alexander Nikolaevich flew to Moscow to fetch the necessary documents for their journey. That was in November. The moment he entered the building where his documents were, it was hit by a bomb which demolished it to its foundations, and Alexander Nikolaevich was killed. Do you remember him? He was a handsome and talented young man. They had everything to live for.

In about a month, if I am not mistaken in my calculations, I shall be able to send you a little money. However, if you are in difficulties, let me know at once and I'll do so without much inconvenience even now. I kiss you and Nita affectionately. I had been thinking of you a long time before writing.

Your
Borya

My address is: Tatar S.S.R., Chistopol, 75 Volodarsky Street, Vavilov's apartment.

1943

To Nina Tabidze

10 December 1943

Dear Nina,

If this letter arrives before New Year's Eve, I hope that it finds you well and prosperous and that everything is all right in your household and in Nita's family.

I cannot forgive myself for not having thanked you till now for the huge apple *Sovkhoz*. What are we going to do about it, Ninochka? I sent you not so much as would buy a packet of cigarettes, if you have not yet given up smoking, and, in return, you send me two thousand roubles' worth of saffron rennets!!

I had a letter from you of one page at the beginning of autumn. Then I left for the front. Meanwhile I am informed that you sent me a telegram. I have not received it. Such things are possible because all these months Zina, Lyonichka, Stasik and I have been bivouacking in four different places which have often changed. For instance, at first Zina lived with the Pogodins, then with the Trenyovs, while I lived with my brother and during the last two or three months with the

Asmusovs. That was because our apartment in Lavrushinsky Lane had been wrecked and half of it taken over by an anti-aircraft company. . . . You can't imagine the trouble it cost me to get rid of them. Now Zina has been living there for over a month (in the lower half of the apartment) and in a few days, after they have put in a telephone, I shall move in there also.

When I came back from the front I did not find Zina in Moscow. She had gone to Sverdlovsk to fetch Adik in order to transfer him to the Moscow Tuberculosis Institute. Your apples arrived on the eve of their return and they were all given to him, poor boy. He has lost a leg and is terribly emaciated. He also has tuberculosis of the spine with constantly festering abscesses. They have to be frequently drained and he has to have blood transfusions. This misfortune has terribly aged and wasted Zina.

Yevgeny Vladimirovich and Zhenya arrived. He is a lieutenant, studies tank building at the Military Academy and is well thought of.

. . . Ninochka, tell Gogla that *Pravda* has asked me twice for translations of his poems. I did not think the first interesting. The second is *very good*, but to translate it means to establish me permanently in secondary, subordinate positions, which in view of the present aggravated struggle for existence and the ambiguity of my present position is harmful, not to say ruinous, for me. Ask Gogla to forgive me and tell him that, if we are alive, I shall one day present him with the same love and attention as in the past.

Now about you. Write to me, Ninochka. I naturally wish selfishly and egoistically that you should be well and strong and live a long time. To begin with, I am trying my best to do the same and I want to meet you while we are both doing our utmost to achieve this aim. But, besides, all that cannot be be described, all that is unheard of, all that has lain on our shoulders, all the unforgettable golden joys and all the mysteries, tragedies and misunderstandings—all this has been done for the sake of people, for the sake of the thousands and thousands of young people from whom we shall one day learn what we did not know and whom we shall have to tell many, many things. We must try to live till that day, Nina.

I hope this equality satisfies you, for you are near and dear to me, just as my nearest and dearest are. You are a member of my family and the more blameworthy am I not to take care of you. Once more, a happy New Year. I kiss you and Nita.

Your
Boris

1944

To Nina Tabidze

30 March 1944

My dear friend Nina,
   I kiss, kiss, kiss you. In my letter I asked you in all sincerity to forgive me for being so far away from you in this difficult time in space, in my troubles, in possible help. And, on top of it all, to let you spend money on us, and as much as you do, crazy darling—how can I possibly allow it or think of it? No sooner had I written this than you sent us a whole caravan of goods, and as soon as I recovered from this shock, a messenger arrived with tea, pounds and pounds of grapes and bottles of champagne from you! I could not with proper civility thank the person who so nobly dragged those heavy loads across Moscow in spite of the difficulties of the present means of communication because you wrote the name of the professor illegibly and the hotel messenger did not know his surname. I'm afraid the professor will form the opinion that I am an ungrateful oaf. The same unfavourable opinion of me will, I'm sure, be given you by Veriko Andzhaparidze, whom I found myself next to in the stalls at the theatre. I have been very busy working lately and this deprives me of the happiness and possibility of

writing to you. I have often been overworked. This ages me outwardly and makes me absentminded. Veriko saw me like that. I didn't recognise her at first. Having recognised her, I couldn't remember her name or who she was. All that must have produced a pitiful and idiotic impression on her. In her account to you she had the right to exaggerate that, too.

Besides, allow me to write with the absolute egoism to which I am entitled. Titian is to me the best model I'd like to follow in my own life, in my attitude towards the earth and poetry, which I have dreamed of in a most happy dream, he is to me almost what he is to you. When I understood from your letter that he was alive, it was my duty to confess to you that I could not believe in this piece of good fortune. During the last years, and especially during the war years in winter, I thought I had got reconciled to the idea that I lived in a large, large building, called the world, where he was no longer to be found. That completely changed reality for me. It was from that realisation that the change Veriko could have noticed in me began. I became more indifferent, more courageous, more intelligible. But that has not only its bad points. That bitterness has disciplined me. If it had been in the Caucasus, I should have said that a wrinkle of vindictiveness had lined my face and had just dried it up a little. But since I am not like that and am myself by the nature of my profession under the influence of the mollifying power that teaches all-forgiveness, it is the contrary that is true. The acceptance of this loss added another few inches to my moral growth and made me taciturn and energetic, just as though I had become something like 'a brother of mercy', immersed in work and gloom.

If what you write to me has any likelihood at all, then luck or God's mercy is even more immeasurable than they strike me as being at every step. I'm simply unable to accept it. I am not prepared for it.

Boris Pasternak at Peredelkino in 1938

Tiflis 1921: Paolo Yashvili, Tamara Yashvili and her father

Left to right: Maria Shanshiashvili, Tamara Yashvili, Nina
Tabidze and Euphemia Leonidze

Tiflis 1933: Nina and Titian Tabidze

September 1943: Boris Pasternak and the critic S. Tregub in uniform

Peredelkino 1946: Boris Pasternak with Nina Tabidze and his son
Leonid

Peredelkino: Boris Livanov with his wife, Boris Pasternak, Simon Chikovani, Besso Zhgenti and Fatma Tvaltvadze

Peredelkino 1958: left to right, Boris Pasternak, his wife and Nina Tabidze. It is not known who the other people are.

Nina, my dear, forgive me for writing all this to you. I suppose it's like monstrously tearing a living body to pieces. Yours, mine, and, in a certain sense, his. The awful thing is that I should have allowed myself to talk about it so precipitately, in such a hurry. But that is because *all the same* his life and yours—in its place in history and nature, in achievement and manifestation—is a poem. In any version, in any circumstances! Mine, too. And it makes no difference whether it is in tears of happiness or of grief. I embrace you warmly.

Your
Borya

To S. I. Chikovani

12 August 1944

Dear Simon,

I have your wonderful *Doubt, Gvantsa, A Swallow's Nest* and *At the Fireplace of Vazha Pshavela*. Mrs. Khitarov gave them to me and I should very much like to translate them. As soon as I get the chance to do them and when they are ready, I shall let you know.

I am, you know, still toying with the idea of paying you a visit, but only in about four or six weeks, nearer to November. If I do go, it won't be to Tiflis, but to some place like Tsinandali or Likani, and certainly with Zina and Lyonichka—you see what extravagant ideas I have and how terrible it would be if after all there would be little likelihood of their realisation. I shouldn't be surprised if for domestic or some other reasons neither Zina nor I find the necessary time for it. In any event, just supposing it were possible, it would be only after I had made the translations from Khitarov's interlinear versions. I should spend the month with you doing some original work, my own, or read and do nothing at all. .... Will you and Marika accept my warm thanks again for everything. Kiss Nina, Georgy Nikolaevich and Euphemia Alexandrovna, and, please tell Grishashvili and Chichinadze that I was glad and thankful to receive their excellent books and, in addition, the fee for the Grishashvili translation.

I embrace you warmly,
Yours,
B. P.

1945

To S. I. Chikovani

3 August 1945

Dear Simon,

I am writing these squiggles to you with my left hand mainly out of affectation. My right hand, thank goodness, is almost well again. I have just finished the rough translation of *Henry IV*. It coincided almost entirely with the disability of my hand and was written with my left hand. Now I shall have to revise it and make a fair copy of it (these versions are never the same, I mean, the rough and the fair copy, they are absolutely different texts). I shall spend another two weeks on it, after which I shall devote all my time to Baratashvili.[1] A group of your academicians sent me a terribly moving and undeservedly flattering telegram. They wished to remain anonymous out of noble modesty. I expect you must know who they are. Thank them warmly for the honour they have shown me. Zina was

---

[1] Pasternak began his translation of Baratashvili on the initiative and with the assistance of Chikovani, who was at the time President of the Georgian Union of Writers.

absolutely delighted and she kept repeating: 'That's true chivalry! That's generosity for you!'

Dear Simon, however much Zina may wish to pay a visit to you with me and the children, I'm afraid it will hardly be possible. Moreover, even if my hand, which God forbid, does not get better (I feel much better), I shall not be able to go to Tskhaltubo even alone by myself. It is too difficult to get away and sacrifice so much time on the journey. I have too much urgent work: work, worries and troubles, and my powers are too limited and I can't get more from anywhere. A journey to Georgia is equivalent to me to a complete liberation from any creative work, a journey to your country means a journey within myself to me, that is, it is my dearest dream as an artist, and I shall never abandon the prospect of its realisation. So it will have to be postponed again only for another year.

. . . If it is possible and convenient to you, I'd like to authorise you to conclude an agreement with the Transcaucasian Government Publishing House for the translation of Baratashvili's works. When you get the advance of 25 per cent, hand half of it over to Nina Tabidze, on whatever pretext you like, but take care she does not find out where it comes from. The other half send to me by post or telegraph. I'm sorry, Simon, to be such a nuisance and burden you with this commission, but you already know the worst about me and you won't think the worse of me because of this. Please, do your best to carry out my request, if it is feasible, especially so far as Nina is concerned. Many thanks for your preliminary remarks about Baratashvili's poems. It's just what I wanted. I kiss you and Marika affectionately. Give my warm regards to Nina, Kira,[1] Nita and Natalya Georgiyevna.[2] I feel as well as ever. I am in excellent

---

[1] K. G. Andronikashvili, a Georgian actress, wife of B. Pilnyak, and sister of the film actress Nato Vachnadze.

[2] Nato Vachnadze.

spirits. Please embrace Leonidze for me and give my cordial regards to Euphemia Alexandrovna.

> Yours ever,
>
> B. P.

To S. I. Chikovani

9 September 1945

Dear Simon,

I have received your telegram about the money. I should never have troubled you, but, frankly, my situation is critical. A short time ago I finished *Henry* (my hand is all right!), translated two poems by Shevchenko, and two days ago I started on Baratashvili. It will be all right, I can already see that.

I examined what had been done before in the same field (Moscow and Leningrad editions) by Spassky, Lozinsky[1] and others (Gaprindashvili good man!—stands out among the rest, incidentally). The attempt to make a rhythmic combination of all the words of the interlinear translation has already been made and is not worth repeating. One has to make Russian poetry of it, as I made it of Shakespeare, Shevchenko, Verlaine and others. This is how I understand my task. One must, if possible, give something light, fresh and unconventional. Many will think it debatable, they will say it is too free a translation of Baratashvili, but that does not frighten me.

I began it about four days ago and I am satisfied with the progress of the work: not only did I have to make no concessions to what I had been writing during the last few years,

---

[1] Sergey Spassky and Mikhail Lozinsky are poets and translators.

but, on the contrary, Baratashvili is particularly amenable to taking a few further steps in the same direction. I hope to finish it quickly. I am translating in strict sequence, one poem after another, and I hoped to let you have half of the collection in about a week, but meeting M. P. Malyshkina, the wife of Balashov,[1] in the street I gave her the first eight pages of the book and asked her to send them to you through Zhgenti, whom they are going to see on their way to Batum. Keep these eight pages for the time being until you receive the rest which are to be numbered in their proper sequence for the Caucasian State Publishing House.

I wonder whether you might not be able to place some of the translations in a Russian newspaper with the approach of the jubilee.

Goodbye, Simon. I kiss you affectionately. Regards to Marika, Nina, Gogla, Euphemia Alexandrovna and others.

Yours,

B. P.

To S. I. Chikovani

24 September 1945

Dear Simon,

I have sent everything off to you today: Baratashvili by registered post, a telegram about it, and now this postcard. Just this moment it occurred to me that *The Fate of Georgia* in its Moscow edition was excellent. It was done by the late Valerian after *The Caucasian Captive* or *The Fountain of Bakhchisaray* in a way no one here could have done it. Antokolsky's introduc-

---

[1] S. Balashov—a well-known reader of poetry.

tion is not bad. Ought *I* to do it? You see, I'd waste a lot of time and work on it. Perhaps we ought to be satisfied with the present translation. Wire me immediately what you think.

Your
B. P.

To Nina Tabidze

1 November 1945

Dear Ninochka,

You see what a miser I am—I am not writing to you on Titian's paper. I feel guilty on many counts. In the first place, I did not thank you properly for your presents and have not sufficiently appreciated their multiplicity and their extent in the frenzied activity before our departure. Having now unpacked everything at home, I was horrified and thoroughly put to shame. Why, the few copecks I left you, have all been spent on this luxury, which moved Zina to tears and made Lyonichka jump for joy and gratitude. How did I let you do such a thing and in my hurry say nothing to you about it? To tell you the truth, I am deeply ashamed and unhappy to have put you to such expense, but I'm convinced that at heart you, too, must feel dissatisfied and grieved by my absentmindedness and lack of attention during the last few days. Secondly, when on the twenty-ninth, on Monday afternoon, I found out that our flight had been postponed (you remember it was after the evening we spent at Leonidze's), I made up my mind to spend my last evening quietly at our hotel and go to see you again without fail. But, as it turned out, I was forced to go to Saguramo and returned to Tiflis at three o'clock in the morning, two hours before we were due to leave for the airport. In Saguramo I arrived practically dead, but I am glad I went. On the return journey Euphemia Alexandrovna sang a lot and taught me a wonderful, complex, labyrinthine Mingrelian song (*Oy, rado*), which I am humming to myself all the time when thinking of her, of you, and of those miraculous two weeks. Once more I am terribly sorry to have missed Nitochka in town. Give her my regards.

What am I to tell you now, Nina? I have paid you a visit and whatever I felt and understood a long time ago, remained, was simplified, and strengthened: defeat turned into conquest, the rare turned into the only one.

. . . It was with a very heavy heart that I tore myself away from you and from the two families that are so near and dear to me, the families of Simon and Gogla, and from the place on the tarmac opposite the hotel where Simon's jeep had been standing for such a long time and where Euphemia had sung, and we had said goodbye. Poor Stepanov and I did not get seats in the plane and we had to sit on our suitcases, and those females kept borrowing money from me and avidly bought and devoured everything they could on the journey and were terribly sick afterwards. I arrived without letting Zina know beforehand by telegram. She turned out to be in Peredelkino, Stasik was at the conservatoire and I had no key to the apartment. I left my things with our neighbours and went to see Zhenya on Tversky Boulevard. There, too, it seemed they were packing their things. Zhenya had to leave for the camp at dawn. I walked along the streets of Moscow with the Mingrelian song in my heart and that heaviness which one experiences when young after a forced and premature separation from people and places which are dear to one. I walked and thought: 'Why did I leave them?' Or better still: I walked and was conscious of having apparently returned to Moscow only with my feet, for with my heart and soul I remained on the little piece of nocturnal tarmac there, not far from you, opposite the hotel, the five of us, myself with the two Chikovanis and Leonidzes.

I am writing to you from Peredelkino where I have just arrived. All are well and send you their thanks and their regards. Zina has gone back to town to see to the repairs (which are still unfinished), there is no fuel for the stove here, and while I have been writing to you the electricity has failed. But everything, I suppose, will be put right. Tomorrow I shall sit down to my principal, routine work. I shall start on the translation of *Macbeth* or *King Lear*. I was very happy in Tiflis. When I was cross because of the feasts night after night and because I was not given time to take a rest, it was not because I was not feeling well—I seemed to have become a nocturnal bird and could cope with it all right, it was because I should have been left longer alone, for then I should really have been able to contribute something to my literary evenings and to the conversations with friends whenever I happened to meet them. As it was, I received a whole world of impressions and, as it were, bathed all the time in a sea of warmth, without giving anything in return. Now I have involuntary and belated pangs of conscience on that account.

I believe that with God's help I shall be among you again in the spring. I shall do so if my work this winter is fruitful, if I prepare an enlarged and more comprehensive programme, including Shakespeare and new things, and give a few large literary evenings in Leningrad, Moscow and Tiflis. So wish me perseverance and success in my work this winter. Once more, thank you, my dear friend, for everything the meetings with you have given me, for the corner of a lane on earth where one can shout 'Nina!' in the evening from under a shady tree at a window on the top floor and feel so much the moment it opens.

I expect to write to Simon and Gogla today, but meanwhile give my regards and kisses to everybody.

Your
Borya

To S. I. and M. N. Chikovani

5 November 1945

My dear, dear friends Simon and Marika,

I wanted to make this letter interesting to you, Simon, and enclose in it my translation of *Doubt*.[1] But goodness only knows what is happening to my rough copies. I only do rough drafts which I do not keep, and my fair copies are not returned by the editorial offices. In short, *Doubt* was not to be found among my papers. It will be found, I hope, in the editorial office of the *Literary Gazette* and I'll send it to you after the holidays as soon as I receive it. The same applies to your poem included in my volume *The Wide Open Spaces*,[2] which cannot be found anywhere and which Kruchonykh promised me to look for in secondhand bookshops.

I keep conjuring up in my mind your house and your clean, bright rooms: the splendid busy city panorama branches out into three parts. One is immediately caught up by a sense of the intelligent, talented, modestly confident atmosphere of your life. The budgerigar bends down its head, screws up its eyes and trills—dr . . . allo!, and my heart contracts with regret to have seen it all and left it.

This journey has brought us terribly close together. I don't

[1] A poem by Chikovani translated by Pasternak under the title *Work*.
[2] A collection of Pasternak's poems published that year.

want to conceal from you that I have long found it difficult to admit that I had to share you and our strengthening friendship with that *mechanical, studied, cheerful enthusiasm* which distinguished our general circle. . . . I am very glad that you are a brilliant and genuine artist, and you and I ought to be close friends.

The writing of these lines has somehow strangely excited me. I wanted to thank you very much and at great length for the Sisyphean labours and innumerable troubles which our general arrival has caused you and for making my stay at your place so fascinating, joyful and precious. You must know yourself that there are very few things in the world which I desire so ardently and with such force as well-earned success and happiness for you and Marika. Please, embrace dear Sergo.[1] My best wishes to you and all yours.

I kiss you,
Your Boris

To S. I. Chikovani

9 November 1945

Dear Simon,

In preparation for going back to town, I have just been sorting out my papers and found *Doubt*. I cannot remember whether it is the final version and I have not got the interlinear translation to check how many mistakes I have made. But I must have made a certain simplification deliberately, and could not help making it, as can be gathered from all my present

[1] S. D. Kladiashvili—a Georgian novelist and a friend and neighbour of the Chikovani family.

translations, for the sake of the clarity of the arrangement of the different parts and the lightness of movement, which means more to me now than any considerations of picturesqueness, emotion and other details. You and I are always so frank with one another that I hope you will write to me and forgive me if you don't like my translation (in the stanza about Vazha Pshavela, especially, I must have made many mistakes, but, as I have told you, I had nothing to check it by). But if my translation is acceptable and is in accordance with your wishes, send it to Korneyev for publication in *The Dawn of the East*.

In my letter to the Kuftins I described my sojourn with you as a mystery play. I cannot find a more appropriate word with which to describe the wave of love and sadness which the memory of those days arouses in me. I must pay you another visit in the spring. Give my regards to Nina, Leonidze, and all those who stayed behind from Moscow, Gudiashvili (him and her), kiss Sergo, Marika and all yours.

I embrace you,
Yours,

B.

1946

To S. I. Chikovani

1 February 1946

Dear Simon,

Have you received my registered letter with the power of attorney and *The Swallow*? I have also translated Leshkasheli and all the three (in addition to *Doubt*, whose title I changed to *Work*). I shall try to have them published in *Pravda*. When you write to me, remind me, please, which of your poems I have translated, for I have never seen your poems of the middle period (with *The Fisherman*) in print and I don't know how many there were and where they have got to. Also, please, tell Gogla to pick out, if he wishes, several of the most simple, interesting and expressive of his small poems, not in any way tendentious, and I will translate them for the proposed Georgian volume, if it comes off. I don't suppose Borodin received your letter, for Yartsev knows nothing of this proposal. Where are you published in Moscow? Where am I to send these new additions? Also ask Leonidze whether the conjectural daguerreotype of Baratashvili has been approved. *Ogonyok* will publish my translations in a separate booklet and it would be nice to have the portrait for it. They asked me for it. But they cannot possibly reproduce this false and touched up one from the 1938 edition, can they? They wanted to telegraph Leonidze about it, but I told them that it is not a simple thing to explain in a telegram, for one could not put it satisfactorily in a few words. If Gogla has some ideas or proposals in this connection (in connection with Baratashvili's iconography), let him write to *Ogonyok*. Perhaps Gogla will write a few words (but very briefly) about his find and what he thinks of it and send the portrait. Or shall we give Lado's portrait? Or the one by a young painter from the Palace of Pioneers (I forget his name, a luminous Baratashvili against a background of a dark-blue Mtatsminda, oils). After an interval of almost ten years, as I was counting the lines in Vazha Pshavela for submission to *The Soviet Writer*, I skimmed through the *Georgian Lyrics* and was surprised to find how marvellously fresh and interesting Paolo still is! There can be no doubt that everything he had a right to demand and expect would have come to pass had he lived. He must have been worn out and crushed by frustration. Tell Nina I dreamed of Titian all night. I dreamed that I spent a night with them somewhere in the mountains which were more like Swiss mountains than ours, in a magnificent, clean and well-furnished house. I lay in a room with a window leading on to a balcony. Day was breaking, but it was still dark in the room with green crimped wallpaper. From the next room Titian was saying something important and nice to me through the open door and as it still seemed to him not sufficiently nice for me, he kept dragging it out while Nina got more and more annoyed with him and kept telling him to hurry up. It was something very bright and—free.

I kiss you and all yours affectionately,

Your

B.

To S. I. Chikovani

15 March 1946

Dear Simon,
Wire me whether you and Marika intend to go to Moscow
now or a little later. I kiss you affectionately for your joint
telegram about the order in which the Baratashvili poems in the
Ogonyok edition are to be published and for your letter, which
arrived earlier. If you are well enough, *look through* the *Ogonyok*
book. I have revised a great many of the poems (*Sergo, The
Infant, The Lonely Soul*[1] and many more) after comparing them
with your copy and I hope greatly improved them. I consider
this revised edition to be the definitive one. Vitya Goltsev
continues to be worried by all sorts of irrelevant points, such as
whether some region might not be left out because of what he
believes to be some inaccuracy in the words of Sol. Leonidze.[2]
But, surely, this is not a State document. What relationship has
this to literature? All this strikes me as terribly inappropriate.
Have a look at my *Ogonyok* version and, if you agree with me
that it can be considered the definitive one, write to Goltsev
about it and set his mind at rest. . . .

I hung about in town the whole month of June because of the
introduction I was writing to my Shakespeare translations. I
was terribly afraid to get stuck in the muddle of pseudo-
scholarly verbosity which every great centuries-old theme
gathers round it and of only adding to this tangled skein a kind
of modified kink. Imagine, it did not happen! I succeeded in
saying in very simple and comprehensible words a great deal

[1] Baratashvili's poems.
[2] Solomon Leonidze—a Georgian statesman, Chancellor of King Hercules
II, a character in Baratashvili's poem *The Fate of Georgia*.

about Shakespeare that I learned when I was translating him, and all this on one printer's sheet! Ask Gogla to show you my translations. I sent them to him. Reply by telegram. Goodbye. Better still, come and don't put off your journey. When you arrive, stay with us in Peredelkino. Plenty of room, quiet.

I kiss you,
Your B.

To G. N. Leonidze

31 March 1946

Dear Georgy Nikolaevich,

Today I received your letter and interlinear translations from M. I. Zlatkin. Many thanks for the one and the other. The interlinear translations contain almost throughout excellent things with deep feeling. Thank you—I shall most certainly use them.

I'm afraid they will probably not get into the Moscow edition of my translations. In my work I have to do one thing then another, and now I have something else to do, while my collection of poems is already being printed. I shall certainly prepare these poems for your Russian editions when the time comes. I am very sorry I did not have them available in February when I was revising something by Baratashvili and translating several things by Chikovani. That was the right time—I did write to you about it a long time ago. But no matter. You have not lost anything, for I hope to make good this omission some time in the future, and whether it will be sooner or later is not really so important.

I am very glad that you and your family have made such a

good recovery from the bad spell of influenza. Because of my advanced age I am no longer subject to such youthful ailments.

Give my cordial regards to Euphemia Alexandrovna and all your family. Zinaida Nikolayevna thanks you for your kind regards and bows low to you.

Yours,
B. Pasternak

To Nina Tabidze

22 December 1946

My dear Ninochka,

This enclosed letter has been lying about for a month, for I intended to send it on by Nina Osipovna Gudiashvili.[1] I wanted very much to see her. She is one of those remarkable women who possess a great deal of individuality, that is, the stamp of personality and humanity is great and strong. But I was busy on the day when I could have met her and next day she fell ill and left for home. The letter remained.

I have been seeing Simon and Marika quite often. They will tell you about us. How are we getting along? I suppose one must not complain, or, perhaps, one must—I find it difficult to judge, so blinded am I by the inner happiness of my existence.

The Chikovanis are leaving tomorrow. When it occurred to me this morning that I should once more kiss you in a letter and write a few words to you, my heart was wrung with anxiety and fear for Nitochka. The uncertainty of her condition worries and depresses me greatly. I am terrified at the thought that I am such an egoist and always so preoccupied with myself. I suppose this is very unfair to our children.

---

[1] Wife of the painter Lado Gudiashvili.

For, you see, even the words of love which, as always, I am going to say to you are merely the expression of the same narrow, personal, subjective intoxication with your house, your street, your city as with some breathing and tremulous flame of a big, big candle, and with you as the sharp tip of this flame and its arrow. Nina, I love you terribly and I am so stupid and inept that you don't know it and that my visit last year did nothing to enlighten.

But why, why do I feel so well in this world, Ninochka? I am ready to weep—it is so startling and inexplicable. In accordance with the logic of delirium, which is a little present in this letter, I have a sort of feeling that you are initiated better than I into my own fate, as though the gods were asking you for your advice, just as though you were a sybil who knows me well, in order to know what to do with me.

Your

Boris

1947

To M. N. Chikovani

25 February 1947

Dear Mariechka,

You have gone, and it is just as if the earth had opened and swallowed you up. I have had no news from you at all.

I suppose that your life must be even more difficult than ours and that you have even less time to spare than we. This alone can explain your long silence.

I hoped that Besso[1] would write to me about the book and tell me whether my introduction was all right. Neuhaus was giving a concert in your town and I thought he would bring me lots of news of you all, but he has only let me have a few precious and warm, but very short, lines from Nina and given me a long account of the two Gudiashvilis, whom, of course, he must have liked as much as they have always delighted me.

You have all—it is all too clear—forgotten me, and if I tell you one or two things about us it is only in the hope that it may

[1] B. A. Zhgenti, at the time editor-in-chief of *The Dawn of the East*.

interest some passer-by under your window and the people living in the apartment next to yours.

Well, to begin with. We were all terribly glad that Simon had been elected a deputy. We congratulate you and him warmly. I have again written a number of poems, and one of them is quite good.[1]

If you do write to me, tell Simon and Besso off for their silence. Persuade Besso to follow his own example as a young man, to remember the days of his youth when he was literate and could read and write, and also exert your influence on *The Dawn of the East* that they should send me money. . . .

Yours,

B. P.

To Besso A. Zhgenti

29 August 1947

Dear Besso,

It seems Nina did not get her ticket and could not leave today. My letter will not reach you as soon as I'd have liked. I should hate to have to re-write *Merani*.[2] My first version turned out light and expressive straight away. I enclose another version of one of the stanzas from memory (I wrote it in a letter which is in Nina's possession in town). . . .

This would fit in very well with the other stanzas.

I kiss you,

Your

B. P.

[1] *Star of the Nativity* included among the *Doctor Zhivago* poems.
[2] *Merani*—a poem by Baratashvili.

1948

To Nina Tabidze

[First half of 1948]

... It is winter, there has been a fall of snow and we have had a long succession of orgies and birthday parties lately, night after night, beginning with Zina's in our house, and followed by others. Livanov[1] is the only man here after my own heart and more or less of my own way of thinking. And my feeling of loneliness grows stronger and stronger in me and reaches a point when I want to howl especially during the hours of abortive gaiety, when the beauty and fruitfulness of the earth are personified by the gleaming table, bathed in electric light, and you are such a sought-after guest, and everyone is so friendly and everyone knows everyone else, and so disgracefully lower than the wines and the food are modern wingless and unimaginative men.

This always affects me closely, hurts me, gnaws at me like a rendezvous that has not taken place because of some outside interference, for love of the future is for me as much a constant

---

[1] B. Livanov, a Russian actor, Pasternak's closest friend.

117

and intimate thing as love of a woman, and I can't do without it. . . .

We have had a rather embarrassing scene. Morozov,[1] one of our invited guests, took offence at Livanov and Chagin[2] and at having been placed far from us at table. When he came to apologise the next day, he complained to me and said that as a boy he had known Rachmaninov, Bely, Serov and others who behaved with decorum, whereas Livanov behaved as if he were a genius without, according to him, having any right to such a claim. I told him that that was what I liked about Livanov, that one had to lay claim to genius, that I fully sympathised with that, that without it I was sick and tired of everything.

Dear Nina, many thanks for placing me in your letter next to Titian and Nita. I do the same to you, I shan't deceive you. Some part of which I write to you, I could have written also to Simon and Gogla. Tell them about me, if they are interested, and kiss them and their wives tenderly and affectionately just as if they were your own brothers and sisters.

Your
Borya

One must write wonderful things, make discoveries, and see to it that wonderful things happen to you. That is life. The rest is rubbish.

[1] M. Morozov, Russian Shakespearean scholar.
[2] P. Chagin, a Russian literary public figure.

1949

To Nina Tabidze

5 April 1949

. . . My oldest passion is art (or what I seem to think is art). I and the circumstances of my life are ruled by it as unambiguously and firmly and with as much clarity as people were once upon a time ruled by religious convictions. This clarity of direction and aim makes everything easy for me. I am always ready for anything and I shall say thank you for everything to fate and heaven.

I kiss you affectionately, dear Ninochka, and with words of infinite gratitude to you and best wishes to all yours I remain your deeply devoted and loving

B. P.

1949

To S. I. Chikovani

24 April 1949

Dear Simon,

Why don't I hear anything from you? How are you? I received a letter from Ivnev and answered him. Natalya Georgievna[1] gave us your regards.

I was just about to write a postcard to tell you that Leonidze was too late to be included in my volume of translations published by the *Soviet Writer*. The volume will include poems by only four authors: Baratashvili, Akaki Tsereteli, Vazha Pshavela and yourself. But Tsereteli will probably receive the same treatment as Gogla. He will be left out because I had only two of his poems and I'm afraid I am entirely to blame for making them uninteresting. In that case there will be left only Baratashvili, Vazha and you, and I will entitle the book: *Three Georgian Poets* or *Three Poets of Georgia*.

I was going to write to you about it on a postcard, but there is a more complicated matter I must discuss with you. A mutual friend of Verkhovsky's[2] and Akhmatova's has just been talking to me on the telephone. Verkhovsky lives under appalling conditons. He had hoped to go to Saguramo, but because of some repairs to the house there his plans fell through. He is a very nice, profound and great man who has been terribly unlucky and his work has a touch of pallor and timidity, as is always the case with people who have had a hard life—I intentionally did not say: with failures. I know we have so much in common that your attitude towards him cannot be different from mine. If you are feeling well enough, please

[1] N. G. Vachnadze.
[2] Yury Verkhovsky, Russian poet and translator.

arrange a permit for him and his wife to spend the whole summer or at least two months in Saguramo. Do that or ask someone in the Union to do it for me. Dear me, I completely forgot: one ought to ask dear Besso to do that. Ask him to arrange this double permit at once and tell them to inform Verkhovsky immediately about it at the address: Moscow, 8, Bolshoy Karetny Pereulok, Apartment 6, Yury Nikandrovich Verkhovsky. I kiss you and Marika. Let me know how you are. I must make amends for hurting Gogla's feelings by publishing my translations of his poems in a separate edition and in the Tiflis edition of my translations. He sent me his interlinear translations giving a very good idea of the mood of his poems —I will certainly do them this summer or autumn.

B.

To N. G. Vachnadze

31 December 1949

Dear Natalya Georgievna,[1]

How talented you are! How rare and excellent is the nature of your talent, how rare and intrepid is its modesty and purity! For, as a rule, gifted people are ashamed of the moral conceptions they have inherited and do damage to themselves and make themselves out to be worse than they are out of sheer timidity. Examples of talent which is true to childhood and home are exceptional and border on heroism.

You are right when somewhere between your characterisation of Mayakovsky and Shengelaya[2] you try to confer these

[1] This letter is in response to Vachnadze's memoirs.
[2] N. Shengelaya, Vachnadze's husband, a Georgian film director.

features of non-hypocritical frankness and youthful freedom from prejudices upon a whole generation. There was a time, indeed, when this could seem to be so; besides, the Russian revolutionary tradition was leading up towards it—the extreme views of Dostoevsky and the Tolstoyan simplifications. But all this is by the way, for this is quite an unnecessary digression.

You write marvellously, as the best writers ought to write, and, which is the chief thing, without detracting from the object of your narrative. A good mastery of the pen, language and a feeling for style tend to draw away from the subject matter and become an aim in themselves, but you did not let style become your master. Once more you were saved by goodness and the long discovered spiritual values which probably lie at the foundation of taste: love of people and gratitude to the past for its brilliance, next to a concern for repaying it with the same kind of beauty and warmth. See how great is your gain in what constitutes the only victory of every genuine work of art!

I am more and more inclined to think that the chief difference between people consists of the difference in the degree of their abilities, and when I cried over some pages of your book (this refers to *The Story of Myself* and *Journey Across Europe*), my tears were aroused by your loftiness, irrespective of what your narrative was about.

You write very well about your father, about the moonlit summer night in Kakhetia, about the sensations of early childhood and love of one's home, about *grdzeli Kakhuri*.[1] You made me cry by the *speed* of the account of your excursion in 1914 to Bergplage, and, indeed, by the *clever compactness* with which so much that is significant and fatal is described in that passage.

[1] A drinking song.

Talent is itself a source of compactness, for it can be viewed with precision and is as obvious as evidence. You can almost see it like a fold in the mind which is as easily visible as a fold in a cloak. I do not believe in anything very big in size or in anything of which there is very much. Women give birth to people and not to cyclopses. Only the inorganic is gigantic, the cosmic spaces of non-existence, the emptiness of death, the deadening principles of ugliness and humiliation.

Another passage that moved me to tears was the way your first marriage, the end of your schooldays and your first job on the stage all took place at the same time. This could be put in one line so thrillingly because life also brought it all together so thrillingly in the past. And once again this absolute correspondence of the gift of life and the gift of the word. When revising the film sequences your desire to correct and re-enact a scene in a new way was very well expressed. Shengelaya's characterisation is very good. Excellent about cities (in your autobiography and in your travels), about Florence, about Berlin. A remarkable feeling (unconscious, of course, it never is otherwise) for the arrangement of the different parts, the instinct for the sequence of events, in what place you tell about what: for instance, it is very good that the story about the children is given before the Trusinsky Gorge. The naturalness of the gradually opening views of the mountain road.

But enough. I congratulate you, and if out of modesty you left the most important things unsaid: how you were the darling of Fortune and how you were loved by the sun that shone upon you and by the earth that carried you (not the earth of Georgia, but the Earth in general, the Earth of the World), it was unnecessary, for the spectator can guess it anyhow from his own overpowering feeling of delight.

I believe in you so much that, when other pages left me cold or reserved because of their subject matter, I thought more than

I would have done in similar cases that it must be my own fault or blindness.

Yes, indeed, a very long time ago I failed to appreciate and understand something in the late Mayakovsky and in many other things. Worst of all are my own limitations, for in those days they overlaid my whole life with an irreparable and impoverishing rigidity. I feel it very strongly now that (I am saying this in all sincerity and without any wish to show off, but also without regret) I am living only with my shortcomings.

From a feeling of deep kinship, which your book aroused in me, I send you my greetings and my gratitude out of my unsuccessful and unjustified life to your successful and victorious one.

Warm regards to Kira Georgievna and kiss Borya.[1]

And, of course, a happy New Year! We shall remember you today with delight. Fatma[2] and Nina will be with us.

Yours
B. Pasternak

[1] B. Andronikashvili, the son of B. Pilnyak and K. Andronikashvili.
[2] F. A. Tvaltvadze, translator of Georgian prose.

1950

To Nina Tabidze

6 April 1950

. . . I have been feeling very well lately, I have been working a lot without difficulty, and there have been no more
changes.

Stasik gives me a great deal of joy, the form of his talent
is very good and very near to me, the form of his attitude to
art and his understanding of it. And of life, too, I suppose. . . .

Over all the radio waves that exist, short and long, I send
you, Nita, Givik and Alexey Nikolaevich,[1] my best wishes.

Garrick[2] tells us wonders about your Givik, about his great
charm and his profound sayings and expresses his regret that
when he was on a visit to Nita the presence of academician
Tsereteli[3] and his conversation with him prevented him from
listening to your little sage.

You must already have seen Akhmatova's poems in *Ogonyok*
or heard about their publication. You remember I showed you

[1] Daughter, grandson and son-in-law of Titian and Nina Tabidze.
[2] G. G. Neuhaus.
[3] G. V. Tsereteli—an Arabic scholar and member of the Georgian
Academy.

125

some of them and not by any means the best. Those I did not know and which she has added to those we had seen are the best. Like everybody else, I am terribly glad of this literary sensation and this event in her life, and the only thing that is unpleasant is that by the same token they have all started looking expectantly in my direction.

But everything she has said now, I had already said twenty years ago,[1] and as one of the first, when such voices were rarely heard and mostly in isolation. Such things are not repeated several times, they either mean something or nothing, and in the latter case no repetition can help matters.

I am very satisfied with my life, with the chance of earning an honest living, and with the serenity of my state of mind. I have never considered myself in any way offended or passed over. If anyone thinks that to a detached observer I may appear to be a 'martyr', then let me say that, first, I am not responsible for anyone's crazy ideas or ridiculous fancies and, secondly, it is sufficient that they who may be interested in such a theory should lift the ban on my books and let me mount the rostrum and this 'semblance of martyrdom', which does *not exist* as far as I am concerned, will disappear by itself. An announcement over the air that I am not a martyr I regard as utterly unthinkable and as sheer idiocy. I am a very proud man, but I should have been a petty and envious person, a bragging nonentity and a young commercial traveller to believe, like any journalist, in the air itself, and in its knowledge of me and its existence for me, when, to be quite frank, I sometimes find it difficult to believe that I interest you or Zina. Besides, if a person suspected of martyrdom declares that he has never had it so good, a suspicion may arise that this declaration has been wrung from him by his sufferings.

[1] A reference to the volume *Second Birth*, containing the poem *Waves* which deals with the theme of revolution and Socialism.

All this is an extremely stupid vicious circle. What sort of person must one be to worry one's head about such things?

It seems to me that all a man's efforts must be concentrated on his activity—successful, bold and productive—and that life should be allowed to do the rest. Happiness in all sorts of higher spheres of existence, such as love (not only love of a woman, but love of one's country or love of one's contemporaries), creative work, and so on, is either given or not given at all, in which case there is nothing to worry about, because one could do nothing about it however hard one tried. Or else it will be a fake. To me, unfaked failure is still more acceptable than faked success. I am sorry, Nina, to have written you such paltry rubbish, but I did it to set your mind at rest if you should be made nervous by some literary gossip.

I kiss you affectionately,

Your

B.

To Nina Tabidze

1 May 1950

. . . Nina, one can be friends and love one another, as you and I, and still remain reasonable and just. I do not know why fate is so good to me. How they overrate me! A huge volume of Goethe's works has just been published and a tenth of it consists of my translation of the first part of *Faust*. I know it is not bad but, you see, neither are almost any of the other translations. Do *they* enjoy a reputation similar to mine? I am turning over the pages of the volume and it is only very occasionally that I come across something clumsy, some hopelessly archaic Slavonic expression. I heave a sigh of relief. Thank goodness, at least one thing is botched. I look up the

127

name of the translator. So-and-so. Well, excellent! Then I come across something exceptionally brilliant. Can it be Kochetov?[1] But no. It seems it is the same poor translator who has a moment ago made me so happy by his nonsense. All of them are such masters that there is no way of escape—disgraceful!

Your

B.

To R. K. Mikadze[2]

18 November 1950

Dear Raisa Konstantinovna,

How charmingly you flirt by beginning your very short letter with the assumption that I probably do not remember you.

I wanted to write to you that very summer in such a way that you would find interesting to read and that my reply should give you pleasure. I went back in my mind to the night when I was about to weep or, indeed, did weep from an overflow of feelings and as a result of your indulgence allowed myself several small breaches of good manners.

That day you were the first to get out of the car when we reached the avenue or even before. This was the beginning of my farewell to the wonderful and magical things I had met during all my travels in Georgia and which cannot be explained only by the South, the mountains, the generous Georgian character, the beauty of the women, the excitement and the elation of the noisy and crowded parties, for it was much more mysterious and profound than all these component parts.

So it is that the significant thing that excites one in nature

[1] A. S. Kochetov, Russian poet and translator.
[2] A Tiflis acquaintance.

and in the world of men has so far not been given a name or word and is still waiting for its definition. It is, indeed, this waiting that is so exciting, like a still unsolved problem or like a flare hanging poised in the sky in expectation of the moment of action.

For instance, such a signal in the history of human activity in Russia that came like a peal of thunder from the depth of the last century was Lermontov. By comparison with Pushkin, the memory of him is highly charged and complicated by something demanding and elusive of which there is almost as much in him as in some keenly felt sorrow or in raw nature. It was only at the end of the century that some ideas in Vladimir Solovyov, something in the symbolists, but chiefly in the work of Vrubel, was the first echo, the first reverberation of Lermontov's sound at a distance of half a century, so difficult is it to grasp and continue what is so exceptional in Lermontov, so unthinkable to respond to his signal with platitudes.

. . . We know of Lermontov that he was a great Russian poet, a great patriot. That is almost the same as saying that Lermontov had arms and legs.

You are probably surprised that I should have started talking about Lermontov. I admit it's a bit irrelevant. But I intended to change the subject later to those unexpected discoveries which I have begun to make even in the best things written by my best friends and which grieve me so much. But I'm afraid this would make my letter much too long. I give up the idea and let what I said earlier remain out of context. Instead I'll write a few words about myself.

Why do you make me a present of such polite phrases as that I am remembered and loved in Georgia, that you have heard a lot about my new works, etc., etc.? I do not say that you do not mean a word of it, but you must admit that one would get a completely different picture if those words did mean something and had any sense. So why should we resort to words in their polite, ephemeral sense? Are we really so poor?

No, my dear, if three or four men in the whole world still know me, there won't be even those in about two years. But why should it upset me? Nevertheless, this obscurity and natural oblivion is not by any means everything. More and more often do I hear utterances by my nearest and dearest and by my most trusted friends who see a decline, an impairment of myself by myself and a retreat into ordinariness in what I have taken an interest in lately and in my present simplicity which I did not acquire so easily. Well, isn't that enough to upset me? If there is suffering anywhere, why should not my art suffer and myself with it? My friends are perhaps right and perhaps not. It is, indeed, very possible that I have gone only a little farther on the road of their own destinies in my respect for human suffering and my readiness to share it.

But do not imagine that I am treating you, who are expecting quite a different kind of talk, to theological soul-saving speeches. I am speaking of the most artistic in the artist, of the sacrifice without which art becomes unnecessary and without which works of art are covered outside with a sprinkling of superficial talent, but inside stick to the ideas which mankind has known well and even outgrown since it emerged from savagery. I'm afraid I have again let myself go goodness only knows how far. You see how I've been carried away in talking to you.

I should like to ask you to do something for me if you won't mind.

I have been intending to write to Nina Alexandrovna Tabidze for some time. I want to write to her very much, but I must write to her about something quite different. She knows it and that is why I am not writing to her, for I cannot find the right words for such a correspondence.

Please, tell her part of the philosophy with which I have assailed you. Tell her that, as before, I live as I like, that I am well, that I am happy to enjoy this right for which I am ready to pay with my life.

You remember that when in Saguramo I spoke of my own home my voice broke and I could not carry on with my speech. Well, I am again talking of the same thing. Zina and I are one inseparable piece of existence just like the way I walk on the floor or see with my eyes. Allowing for this corner-stone fact, I love Nina Alexandrovna more than anyone else in the world. This you need not tell her, this you can conceal from her. I kiss your hand.

Your

B. Pasternak

To Nina Tabidze

5 December 1950

Dear Nina,

You must have received my empty and hasty letter, but do not be in a hurry to answer it. About the tenth of December, that is, in about a week, I hope to transfer a little money to you so that you shall not feel the pinch before Christmas and the New Year. Answer me during the holidays.

I really am all right as I believe I wrote to you. I should probably write better and more quickly if I did not have to translate such ridiculous stuff as the second part of *Faust*.

I am more than at any time satisfied with my life and do not desire any changes. More recently a great deal around me has seemed terribly trivial. If anyone really wanted it my life could have been changed by something more far-reaching than the magnanimity extended to it. But that is the business of the great soul unknown to me. As for me, I cannot behave otherwise and this irreversibility fills me with happiness.

I kiss you affectionately,

Your

B.

1951

23 February 1951

Dear Nina,

For over a week now the marauding family of Pasternaks has been rapaciously and shamelessly devouring your supplies, flinging themselves upon the sweets and swallowing them, eating the apples, drinking the wine, which equals Beethoven in inspiration, and drowning all the dull products of their own cuisine in your all-transforming pomegranate juice.

But the *pièce de résistance* was of course the boy who brought all these goods—young G. L. Asatiani.[1] What charm! I at once thought how elated and hampered Asatiani and Tina Kalistratovna must feel to have such a son. Something here reminds me of my attitude towards Stasik, when the presence of a member of the family outgrows the ancestral framework of home, just as if someone were all his life on a visit and every day were a holiday.

I am glad to have received news and a letter from you. I was beginning to be worried. One night I dreamt of you and the

[1] A Georgian critic, at the time a student at Moscow University.

133

actress Giatsintova (I had spoken to her on the telephone earlier). Both of you were elected deputies, you were receiving petitioners, and I saw your portraits, Nina, everywhere. . . .

Not a day passes without my realising in some new way the advantages I derive from the fact that fate has not spoilt me by outward success, that it has treated me with apparent severity, that I have always lived productively, by practical work, and advanced in my trade, and was not busy with carrying about a questionably acquired name—ought I not to thank heaven for all that?

. . . One rainy evening I was escorting Akhmatova home from some place. We walked arm in arm. As I was telling her something about Spassky, water came pouring down on us from the gutters of some houses. At the climax, when the shower of water was particularly heavy and my praise of Seryozha particularly high, I squeezed her arm tightly as I pulled her from under a waterfall and she said, 'But I am not Seryozha Spassky!' That was delightful.

Your

Boris

To Nina Tabidze

15 April 1951

Dear Nina,

Once more I have lived through all this in my mind as in the days of Baratashvili, even before Zina's return. When I received their telegram: 'Leaving on Wednesday 28th', etc., my heart sank, just as though I had been in their place and the train had begun moving under my feet, and the enchanting city, with its enchanting, gorgeous people and all that six-day-long splendid, dream-like spectacle, had sailed away far into the distance never to return. Nina, my best friend, my joy, I am ready for anything at any moment. But if I were no more, my life would be left behind, such a happy life, for which I am so grateful to heaven, a life which, like a book, was full of such quiet, concentrated meaning. What was the chief and fundamental thing about it? The example of my father's work, love of music and Scriabin, two or three chords in my own writing, night in the Russian countryside, the revolution, Georgia.

I was glad to satisfy myself that you and yours are so near to Zina, a straightforward person who hates all wild enthusiasm and affectation. She talks of you, Nita, Givik and Alexey Nikolaevich as she does of her own flesh and blood, as of Stasik and Lyona. . . .

I was completely bowled over by the splendour and magnificence of the reception Georgy Nikolaevich gave to Zina, his words of welcome and his gift (a cask of that legendary Fina). I was even more touched by the cordiality and attention of Maria Alexandrovna and Alexander Ilyich Shanshiashvili. We had never been on intimate terms just because I was always stopped short by my immense respect for them, and suddenly their affectionate reception of Zina, Lyona and Gala[1] (I say nothing of Stasik because he has his own deserts), and that party, flowers and the send off and the pies. Many thanks to them, to you, to everyone.

Neither in my note to Georgy Nikolaevich nor in my few lines to A. I. Shanshiashvili could I find or express anything like the feelings and the pictures that swept over me and flashed through my mind under the influence of Zina's stories about them. These reminders transferred me to the places of the described events, and in my mind I rushed with them all in the dusk, after getting up from the table at Shanshiashvili's, to the station through the city in the evening, the party still fresh in my mind and my head dizzy with wine.

[1] Wife of Stanislav Neuhaus.

I should like to say a lot to both of them, and if the above lines say nothing, do not communicate anything I have written to them and give them my regards in your own words instead.

We had visitors a short while ago: Natalya Georgievna, Akhmatova, the Livanovs, Fatma Antonovna, Chikovani, the Chagins, etc. I dedicated the evening and everything that happened in the course of it (there was an electricity cut and we lit candles) to the absent Leonidze. Natalya Georgievna will tell him about it.

I kiss you affectionately, Nina,

Your B. . . .

To G. N. Leonidze

15 April 1951

My dear and great friend, Georgy Nikolaevich,

Thanks, thanks, thanks! Oh, I've got so many things to tell you! I'd better not start. For everything is bound to come out anyhow since I'd like to include everything and speak about everything.

But, then, all this is so natural. How else? Zina arrived and went on and on telling me of the things that happened to her during her visit. And once more there stands before my eyes the whole of that indescribable Tiflis fairy-tale and the sensations accompanying it enter like a sea into my soul. I want so much to turn them over to you, to the voice of that sea, to its roar, its creative interpretation!!

It would have been the tale of the white bull-calf, told to everyone so many times already, and I'd have had to write *The Waves* again and the poem about the artist, in which I had you in mind,[1] and then recall my visit in the winter of 1933.

[1] According to Leonidze the reference is to the poem *The Artist*.

Oh, how natural and real it was! That on the very first evening of my arrival the cup of ecstasy should have been filled to the brim and that someone should have been its last drop! That in a city built in the European fashion with its extraordinary population, clearly and nervously delineated in Southern style, at night, against a thick network of fast falling snow (the first snow!!),[1] a figure I had never seen before should have passed rapidly, and everything should have risen to a climax and all my strength should have been drained out of me with sheer delight! That the very next day I should suddenly have realised who it was,[2] and that the emotion aroused by that admonitory force, inhibiting and slightly tragic, like every reminder, should have emanated from your life, from your house!

Oh, Leonidze, Leonidze, how big, how solemn, and how beautiful it all is!

Zina speaks with admiration of your handsome grandson. I am deeply sorry to hear that poor Tina[3] is ill (but Nina wrote to someone here that she was a little better?). Is Euphemia Alexandrovna still in hospital? I wish them both with all my heart a speedy return home.

You are hurt that I should not have answered your New Year's telegram. Well, of course, it wasn't nice, but I made no exception for you: I did not reply to several others. It was not because of bitterness or resentment that I refused to celebrate the New Year and afterwards, a month later, my own birthday. I don't know myself what made me do it and I cannot explain it. There must be a great deal of the feminine, of the passive, in my character. I am, of course, active, industrious, persevering. But I don't know how to undertake anything in

[1] This apparently is an allusion to Leonidze's poem *First Snow*.
[2] Euphemia A. Leonidze.
[3] Leonidze's youngest daughter.

life, I don't like 'to take steps'. Just as I have given myself up several times into the hands of life and into the hands of serious work, so, in the long run, all that is left to me is to give myself up into the hands of death. That is all my programme. It is still the same. No one can tell whether anything is destined to happen to me before I take leave of you. But how lovely, how solemn, how perfect this is, too!

I kiss you and Euphemia Alexandrovna's hand affectionately. And, yes, thank you for the barrelful of that wonderful drink!

Your

B.

1952

To G. N. Leonidze

9 April 1952

Dear Georgy Nikolaevich,

When Elena Davidovna[1] gave me this interlinear translation,[2] I told her that I was busy translating from languages I know and that, besides, apart from *Faust*, my time will be taken up completely by prose.[3] I like some passages of the interlinear translation, describing the muddle and complexity of the past and the present, Baratashvili's death and his apotheosis. I realised that no translator, not even myself, could guess which lines in the text of the interlinear translation are Baratashvili's and which are yours, and, even if you marked them, no translation could suggest what distinguishes the one from the other to enable the Russian reader to separate them and to understand which echoes which and which crisscrosses which or which interlaces with which. I have completely given up any idea of providing rhymes for this interlinear translation.

But Euphemia Alexandrovna telephoned us. Her difficulties and doubts about how she should deal with doctors and illnesses,

[1] E. D. Gogoberidze-Lundberg, translator and literary critic.
[2] Leonidze's poem *N. Baratashvili*.   [3] *Doctor Zhivago*.

139

her calm, conciliatory and jocular tone regarding all these matters produced on us, on Zinaida Nikolaevna and myself, an impression of something near and dear, as though her troubles were our own. It was then that the interlinear translation revealed itself as something that concerned her closely, and I began, submissively like a medium, to reduce it to some poetic order. When Euphemia Alexandrovna and Fatma Antonovna stayed with us, I told her that I felt as though she were making the translation and I were dissatisfied with her work.

You see, it really turns out to be a kind of feeble absurdity, as I foresaw, and not only because I did it so badly, but also because it could not be done at all. It is only in the original, only in the sound of the Georgian language that a Georgian ear recognises the familiar inserted passages from Baratashvili which he knows by heart and experiences these encounters and disturbances. No translation into any language can reproduce this interplay of moods.

Nevertheless I carried through this attempt, foredoomed to failure, to its end and I am presenting you with these pages unofficially and just as a curiosity, without any obligations or consequences, with no ulterior motives, either monetary or ambitious, in connection with them. It is not a translation and if you still think that your poem can be translated (the interlinear translation gives only a partial and very feeble idea of it) commission someone else to do it. My translation must not be published, in my own interests. Someone belonging to the petty breed, who loves to catch out the great in the small and regards this as his good fortune, may fasten on to it as an indisputable failure acknowledged by myself.

When you are in Moscow come and see us and bring Euphemia Alexandrovna and Fatma Antonovna with you.

I embrace you,

Yours B. P.

Would it be possible to abridge everything in the translation by throwing out all the inexpressive, vague and repetitive stanzas? What do you think? Towards the end it seems a little better, the idea springs to life.

To S. I. and M. N. Chikovani

14 June 1952

My dear Simon and Mariechka,

How are you and what's your news? Are you planning to visit Moscow soon and when shall we see you? Tomorrow we are leaving for the country and, if you have not changed your minds (about your arrival in spring), we shall await you in Peredelkino.

Since your departure I have been feeling well all the time, especially during the last month, when I progressed a little (one new part) in my prose.[1] I read it about a week and a half ago to a circle of close friends, of whom you are part and whom you have met at our place, the Zhuravlyovs, Akhmatova, Scriabin's daughter and others.

Approximately during these days of my feverish work (I can work only in a hurry and behind schedule, by fits, that is when my work is true bliss to me), Euphemia Alexandrovna arrived. When after that savage period of reading I was once more a human being, we arranged a meeting by telephone, and she spoke so intelligently and calmly about her illnesses and difficulties, with such traits of a mother with a large family and the head of an important and complicated life, that I felt that I had to do something with my own hands for her world

[1] *Doctor Zhivago.*

141

and her home, and I undertook to express rhythmically and in rhymes a poem by Georgy Leonidze on the death of Baratashvili. It is composed of an alternation of the author's verses with extracts from Baratashvili's poems and I can only suppose these interruptions and contrasts become clear only in Georgian and are lost in an interlinear translation. It is untranslatable. Last winter when Elena Davidovna gave me this interlinear translation I refused to try to do anything with it in spite of a few very good passages which express the ultimate enfeebling bitterness of Baratashvili's life and death, and a few stanzas which show how everything had undergone a change. In spite of these passages of real sincerity, the interlinear translation has so many inconsistencies, obscure passages and repetitions that much remains incomprehensible. It would have been illogical and, perhaps, even unscrupulous on my part to undertake the translation, but I undertook to do it all the same. The result (of *my* work!) was such an absurdity that even so kind and tactful a man as Georgy Nikolaevich could not possibly accept it.

It was a repetition of the fable of *The Hermit and the Bear* with its moral that an obliging fool is more dangerous than an enemy, and I turned out to be that fool. And, indeed, Zina, Euphemia Alexandrovna, Leonidze and myself had no more joy of all that than if I had been knocking my head against a wall for two days. It is obvious that I must never again translate from interlinear translations but only from languages I know.

Oh, if only I could send one little part of my calm and satisfaction with life to you, though why should I? I expect you, too, have no lack of feelings you would like to share with your friends. But you may depend on it you will not find anywhere a more thickskinned rhinoceros than I. Nothing seems to have any effect on me.

Of those who have read my novel the majority are dissatisfied. They say it is a failure and that they expected more from me, that it is colourless, that it is not worthy of me, but I, acknowledging all this, just grin as though this abuse and condemnation were praise.

I kiss both of you affectionately,

Your

B. P.

Listen, Madame Chikovani and Monsieur Chikovani: everyone misses you in the North. Come and stay with us in Peredelkino!!!

All mine send regards to all yours.

Your

B. P.

I am very fond of you both. Don't be afraid of anything, don't be upset by anything.

To S. I. and M. N. Chikovani

2 July 1952

My dear Simon and Mariechka,

I shall be in town on Tuesday and I have a faint hope that I shall find a letter from you at our flat. But, even if it is not so, I should very much like to have a little talk with you now.

After sending off my spring letter to you I learnt from Fatma Antonovna that you had been seriously worried lately by certain distressing circumstances. Nina, who arrived a month later, brought the good news that your circumstances had resumed their normal course.

I am very glad of it, though I feel that you are an artist with quite a special star, with special tasks and special merits, that before that feeling all the vicissitudes of your life are pushed

143

into the background, and that the creative image of a man possessing such original gifts, a man who has sought so much and has found and produced so much, will never suffer from any trials that may beset him, but will grow and be enriched with every change. At our next meeting I shall tell you more on the same theme.

Once more the days of Nina's departure are drawing near and, as every summer, I am saddened by the approaching parting. She found us in good health, Lyona grown up, a new human being come to life, Stasik and Galina's daughter Marina. This summer we have had a lot of sunshine and I spend almost all my time in the kitchen garden and do no work.

At the beginning of summer, as I wrote to you, Euphemia Alexandrovna was here, then Georgy Nikolaevich arrived with his daughters. I spent a pleasant time with him but saw him only once. I saw Euphemia Alexandrovna and Nestan more often. New untapped deposits of the warm friendship existing between our two families were discovered and found their development in the way Euphemia Alexandrovna, Nestan, Zina and Lyona rushed off, all four of them, to Leningrad to spend the stock of their mutual, warmhearted friendship in tireless sightseeing and other tourist pastimes.

I, too, tried to express, in conversations at table, something I felt in my heart towards each of them, but so unsuccessfully that they all kept turning away.

I was no more successful, as I wrote to you, in my translation of Leonidze's poem on Baratashvili, and later of three poems by Tsereteli, and I felt ashamed when Euphemia Alexandrovna and Zina spoke of this dull rubbish with approval. . . .

I kiss the two of you. Warm regards to all our friends and acquaintances.

Yours,

B. P.

To Nina Tabidze

6 September 1952, Saturday

Dear Nina,

I have suddenly learnt from Stasik, who has just arrived, that he and Milochka stayed in your room and that Nita wasted four or five days of her busy and fully occupied life on them. I am particularly sorry for Nita, for I never sacrifice my free time for anybody. I was about to express my thanks to you and her in this letter, when I learnt from Zina and Lyona, who un-expectedly arrived from town for the week-end (it is Saturday now), that Nitochka had arrived in Moscow and had visited them ten minutes before the arrival of their taxi. Zina had begged her to come with them to Peredelkino, but she said that she had some business to see to and promised to come tomorrow, on Sunday. Here I interrupt my letter and shall continue it after having seen her.

8 September, Monday

It is strange, but the night after that letter, from Saturday to Sunday, I did not shut my eyes for a second, that is, I lay all night without a wink of sleep. I was about to fall asleep when the barking of Mishka under the window awoke me several times and all my capacity for sleep was ruined. This distressed me, for we were expecting visitors on Sunday and I wanted to receive them with all my faculties at full strength and not as an unslept phantom. Besides, I did not altogether believe in Nita's promised visit, and the night before, before my insomnia, I decided to get hold of her by telephone through Fatma Antonovna and, if unsuccessful, to go to Moscow to fetch her and bring her to Peredelkino to dinner. I had to give it all up because of my somnolent listlessness, but, as always, worked all morning in the kitchen garden.

The first to arrive was Nita with a female friend. The photographs Zina and Lyona brought with them from their trip do not give a good likeness of her. The whole charm of her face is expressed in the way it is alive and changes when she speaks or is surprised or laughs or in an outburst of powerful emotion. I looked at her and could not help admiring the fire that animated her, the fire of wit and nobility, and the fire of her independent manner of thinking and feeling. After a completely sleepless night, in the condition I had been in that day, that was the only thing I could do to fill the slow hours of a hot day: to dig round and mulch the apple trees with earth and manure and to look at Nita and listen to her. But the apple trees I tended with dry eyes, while Nita I admired through tears, which clouded my eyes not only when we recollected something together, and my voice broke and I was unable to speak, but also every time Nita showed her shrewd understanding of life and her attitude towards it and when it made me happy that she was like that. I was sorry she saw me looking so pale and tired and so indifferent to everybody else at the table. Shortly before that, when Zina was away and when I was in charge of the house, and everything was quiet and shipshape, with insufficient provisions, the Livanovs arrived and spent the night in my room, and Fedin spent the evening until three o'clock in the morning with us (I had to get the wine from our neighbours because of their late arrival after the shop was closed). But the love and the thoughts these people brought with them! I spent the time so interestingly, in such exciting conversation! Just as though my own life in their person entered into me and said a lot of necessary and joyful things to me! It is a pity Nita did not see them or someone like them. Why, they even forgot what was going on outdoors and it was only Anna Nikandrovna who, happening to come in, remembered that below the apple trees were laden with apples and went downstairs to have a look at them. At table it was as if we were in some basement drinking den, and I felt too weak to remind them that we ought to eat and drink in the garden. I am sorry Nita saw me so indifferent to people and perhaps mistakenly assumed that I was so terribly lonely—it is not so.

Now, to finish this letter let me say this. Many reasons, Nita herself, her likeness to her father, the innumerable incidents of the time which we had recalled, reminded me again how terrible and how partly ineffectual my life was without Titian. But how am I to tell you something else, too? Almost as frequently I caught myself thinking that, perhaps, you and Nita would not have been so near to me, that you would not have been my equals, if your life had been easy, if you had a car, if you had been spoilt and corrupted by tittle-tattle and idleness. I appreciate the fact that you have to work, because I am a man who is accustomed to his day being filled with work as it is filled with the sun and the sky, I am a man who is wholly devoted to a given task and a single purpose and not to some homeopathic part of it. But enough of that.

Tell Leonidze's family that oblivion reminded me of them, two cases of forgetfulness. First, Zina forgot to send you the photos taken in Peterhof (the photographer touched up Lyona and Zina, but Euphemia Alexandrovna and Peso[1] got out of focus and spoilt them—I don't like these photos). Second, Euphemia Alexandrovna and Peso left a mirror in their Leningrad hotel room and it was returned to us in Peredelkino. What an amazing business! I kiss them all. You have quite an exceptional daughter, Nina. I kiss you affectionately.

Your

B.

[1] Pet name of Leonidze's elder daughter Nestan.

1953

To Nina Tabidze

17 January 1953

Ninochka, I am still alive, I am at home. Oh, there are so many things I have to tell you.

I have left your overwhelming letters, charged with the liveliest affection and solicitude, unanswered, the letters of three periods, first those you wrote in the autumn in which you told us about Nita and about how you were re-reading my books, then those in which you told Zina that you were ready to come to Moscow to help her, and, finally, the last ones with your appeal to Zina to trust you as her sister. . . . How can I thank you? What words can I find to show my gratitude?

This is what I want you to know—you, Simon and Marika, Georgy Nikolaevich and Euphemia Alexandrovna. I repeat it to my closest, closest friends.

Some may think: 'Yes, all those fine words, idealism, creative work, and all those speeches and toasts are all right for so long and no longer, at table with friends, until the first trouble and the first serious trial. Let us see what will be left of it at the first collision with the inevitable. . . .'

148

When it happened and I was taken away and then spent the first five hours in the reception room and afterwards a night in the corridor of an ordinary, huge, and overcrowded city hospital, I was seized by such a wonderful feeling of calm and bliss in the intervals between loss of consciousness and attacks of sickness and vomiting.

I kept thinking that in the event of my death nothing inopportune or irreparable would happen. Zina and Lyonochka would have enough to live on for six months, after which they would look round and find something to do. They will have friends. No one will treat them badly. The end will not come to me by surprise, in the middle of my work, before something is finished. The little that could be done among the obstructions caused by the events of our time has been done (the translation of Shakespeare, *Faust* and Baratashvili).

All about me everything went on as usual, things stood out so vividly, shadows fell so sharply! A mile-long corridor with bodies of sleeping patients plunged in darkness and silence, at the end of which a window looking out into the grounds through which one caught a glimpse of the inky haze of a rainy night with the reflection of the glow of the street lights of Moscow behind the treetops. This corridor, the green glow of the lampshade on the table of the night-nurse, the stillness, the shadows of the nurses, the proximity of death behind the window and behind my back—all this taken together was, by its concentration, such an unfathomable, such a superhuman poem!

At a moment which seemed to be the last in my life, I wanted more than ever to talk to God, to glorify everything I saw, to catch and imprint it on my memory. 'Lord,' I whispered, 'I thank you for having laid on the paints so thickly and for having made life and death the same as your language— majestic and musical, for having made me a creative artist, for

149

having made creative work your school, and for having prepared me all my life for this night.' *And I rejoiced and wept with joy.*

Now you will nevertheless ask me how I am, where I am and how I am feeling. I can feel my heart all the time: when I move, when I talk, and even when I am writing these words. They tell me that this will go on for a long time and then it will pass.

My chief trouble is caused by the deposits of salts on the cervical vertebrae (spondylitis), somewhat relieved last summer when I moved about a lot and no longer felt it, but it recurred and deteriorated quite monstrously because of my immobility during the two months of lying on my back. As I felt it only when they lifted me up, this discovery poisoned the joy of my recovery.

Chikovani and Leonidze inquired by telegram about my health and sent their New Year's greetings, Euphemia Alexandrovna and Peso sent Lyona birthday greetings. Many thanks for this remembrance and warmth.

I shall find it difficult now to write to each of them separately: every time I talk or write I feel a painful lump rising to my throat (this, I believe, is a symptom of stenocardia).

Tell them about my sensations in hospital. They ought to know that not because they are my close friends, not because they are people I love, but for a more important reason: they ought to know it because they are the not so numerous representatives of the world which I subjected to a test in those hours when death was hovering over me and which grew so big in my mind and received such a confirmation.

Zina is feeling better. She did a tremendous lot for me and saved me. Her liver is enlarged and painful. We shall both go to a convalescent home for a month, but we don't know exactly when or where.

I kiss Nita, Givik and Alexey Nikolaevich. Do not judge my letter too severely. I still find it difficult to write. It's bad for me, it's forbidden.

Your

B.

To Nina Tabidze

7 July 1953

Dear Nina,

Why aren't you coming? Even now I am doing something I shouldn't, giving in to my desire to write to you and shirking a rush job. Now, after my thrombosis, all work has become a rush job to me.

My dear, dear, dear friend, you know that for a long time I have not believed in the possibility that T.[1] was alive. He was too great, too exceptional a man, who shed light all around him, to be hidden, for the signs of his existence not to have filtered through any bars. Your revived hope that we might perhaps see him infected me, too, for a moment.

If he is alive, he will most certainly return to your life and mine. It would be an unthinkable piece of good fortune: this, just this and nothing else would have completely changed my life. It would, indeed, have been the reward of fate, the compensation, which never, never falls to my lot when, after an enormous expenditure of feelings and nerves, I crave something of equivalent value, and no amount of money, no amount of pleasures, nothing in the world, could compensate me for my lost powers.

Come, we have been waiting for you for a long time. I cannot write to you or even telegraph you decently because of my rush job. I am sure you do not find me in my letters. They

[1] Titian Tabidze.

must seem cold and absent-minded to you. Come and stay with us just out of curiosity, to see how I have changed for the worse. I do not write to you anything about myself or us on purpose: you will find everything out for yourself on the spot. Kiss Nita and Alexey Nikolaevich and send our kisses to Givik in the country. It always hurt me when you wrote your golden letters with your heart's blood, like your last letters to Zina and me about Stasik, for there are no answers of equal significance to such letters. Come, Ninochka! I'll remind you how much I love you and that I am still a man with whom one can talk—you have forgotten it.

I kiss you affectionately, affectionately, affectionately.

Your B.

Give my regards to the Leonidze family, to the ladies and to himself. What an awful misfortune, what a shattering blow was the death of Natalya Georgievna![1] Such talent, the face of life itself at its best, such a beautiful woman! If I could spare the time, I should have liked very much to write to the two Chikovanis—to him and to her. They are people whom I'd like to meet many times in life, if I live long enough. I believe in Simon's future.

Your B.

To G. N. Leonidze

5 September 1953, Saturday

Dear Georgy Nikolaevich,

If I do not see you today as Zina promised me on her return from town (she said you would be visiting the Leonovs in Peredelkino and then come to see us), I shall be the only one to

[1] N. G. Vachnadze.

blame. I know that you rang us many times in town, I do not doubt your desire to see us, and I want to see you very much myself. I should have shown greater initiative and should have arranged a meeting myself. The fault lies with my reduced activity of recent months and a certain general alienation from what is happening in literature and from literary circles.

But all that does not matter a bit. I hope you will come and see us another time. I'll be in town, we shall meet and everything will take care of itself. I'm writing this to you to put your mind at rest, so that you should not feel any embarrassment or regret that we did not meet. I repeat, you're in the clear. It is I who should have been more enterprising and more insistent.

Now, in the autumn, I am alone in the country, except during the week-ends when Zina and Lyona join me here. I am thinking how wonderful it would be if Nina had stayed with me during this month—but that's just a dream. Quite apart from her job, which would not have allowed her to do that, she would, of course, have been bored to tears when forced to share my carefully regulated rigid regime of work, my daylong silence and 'opening my lips' only at dinner and in the evening. But I should, of course, have been in the seventh heaven. She is my greatest, my very greatest friend, as you know, and in her company I lived and worked wonderfully.

Still, even now during those not infrequent days when autumn blows darkness, cold and loneliness in my face, I overcome these attacks of depression by our only means of salvation—work. And I am stoking my stove.

If only you knew how I admire your household, your life!

I kiss the hands of all of them in the person of Euphemia Alexandrovna and embrace you.

Your

B. P.

To Nina Tabidze

... Ever since my childhood I have nourished a timid feeling of adoration for woman, all my life I have remained stunned and stupefied by her beauty, by her place in life, and by my pity of her and fear for her. I am a realist who has a thorough knowledge of the earth not because, like Don Juan, I have frequently had a lot of fun with woman on earth, but because since childhood I have gathered pebbles from under her feet on the path she has trodden.

The few women who have had an affair with me were magnanimous martyrs, so unbearable and uninteresting am I 'as a man', so often am I incorrigibly and inexplicably weak, so much do I not know myself even now and know nothing of this aspect of life. They are perhaps touched by the fact that some poor human being has in spite of everything dragged himself to them from far, far away, a being devoted to them since childhood and since childhood shaken and racked with pain for them, and also shattered on the way by the high-minded war he has fought for them. Perhaps, too, they are touched by the strange purity, always familiar to women from memories of their own childhood, which has encompassed so many things in life, and still remains to this day. . . .

Now, secondly—art. In *Resurrection* and *Anna Karenina* Tolstoy shows how Nekhlykdov and, in the second case, Vronsky, who has gone to Italy with Anna, buy all the necessary art accessories—canvases, pencils, brushes, paints, in order to paint pictures, but somehow nothing seems to come right, either the mood is wrong or the weather is not good enough, and beside them is shown a man who is mad about painting and who contracts tuberculosis because of his dedication to art, a poor, simple man. . . . It is this gentlemanly, amateurish, idle attitude towards the whole world of self-sacrifice and hard work, which I know so well and to the service of which I am devoted, that surprises and repels me. I saw something in life that had some connection with great men. It must be remembered that this kind of upper class idea of art, an art for young ladies and the cinema—does not belong to my repertoire. I do not say that one ought to hang anyone who is not a genius, but in that case one's approach and one's standards must be quite different. . . .

Oh, how I wish that *Faust* would be published soon so that I could send it to you. You will be the only one in Tiflis to whom I shall present it, so few copies will I get. A good thing, too! Let them read it out of your dear hands. Tear the book in two, take the first part yourself and give the second part to Euphemia Alexandrovna. The first part deals with earthly love and the second with heavenly. She is peerless—E. A. is—isn't she? When I was translating the second part, Helen involuntarily acquired her features; in the text I gave her words which E. A. might have uttered. I should have liked to inscribe her copy thus: Read what Goethe writes about you in the second part. What do you think? Ought I to write such an inscription?

Ninochka, Khitarova[1] of the State Literary Publishing House wanted to give me interlinear translations of three of Chikovani's poems. I consider him to be one of the most interesting poets of the contemporary world and I have proved how much I love and value him in different ways. But I am immersed in my prose novel and even the little poetry that still enters my head I do not develop thematically, as I did last summer, but either discard or remember without writing it

[1] S. M. Khitarova, at the time editor of the State Publishing House.

down in a rudimentary, figuratively unconcentrated and un-condensed form, so much do I consider my prose novel my sole business and do not allow myself to be distracted from it and to be squandered on poetry. . . .

. . . I shall write down for you the incidental poems I men-tioned in passing. These poems are not a patch on the others, they are second-rate because they are only tender and musical, whereas poetry ought, in addition to music, to contain painting and meaning. They are very short and I have brought them together under the title: *Lullabies*. You can let anyone you like read the poems you have as well as these.

. . . Nina, it is a warm, cloudless autumn day, twelve o'clock, the sun is pouring in through the wide, six-panelled window, and I am sitting with you in Peredelkino and, instead of work-ing, wasting your time by this endless letter, my Nina, my joy, my sister.

I kiss you endlessly,
Your
B.

1954

To Nina Tabidze

30 April 1954

Dear Ninochka,

I am answering you in haste because I am up to my eyes in all sorts of work. . . . I am sorry not to have written to you for such a long time, thinking mistakenly that, being too busy yourself, you wouldn't be writing, either. In the meantime, it seems you had sent me a letter by a friend. We never received such a letter. As regards Lyona's collar, shoulders and sleeves, I am authorised to state that Lyona has not anything of the kind, but that he does have a nose, eyes and hair. What do you want it for, Nina? When will you stop doing crazy things?

. . . Since you like to carry out pleasant commissions, I have a request for you. I have had no copies of *Znamya* till quite recently. I only found out the day before yesterday what I looked like in print.[1] I also read Chikovani's *The Way of Friendship* which is the first item in the journal. A very vivid,

---

[1] A reference to Pasternak's ten poems from *Doctor Zhivago* published in *Znamya*.

true, lifelike description of a journey which makes a real impression, like the prose of a good novelist, very ably rendered by Mezhirov. Very good. Fine lads both. . . .

When Simon was here, I was still unable to see clearly, either myself or him, and I was silent. He might have got the impression that I did not like his poem. Incidentally, in *Znamya* they had put aside my author's copies, but some students came, said that I had sent them, and took them away.

I kiss you,
Your

B.

1955

To Nina Tabidze

7 September 1955

My dear Nina,

Many thanks for everything. Viva has just given me your letter, I read it and make haste to write a few words of thanks to you. . . .

In her letter Zina mentions 'miracles of hospitality' (those are her own words), which were performed by Georgy Nikolae-vich. Viva added many particulars in her account. I see it all in my mind's eye, I see you all again with your families, I see Euphemia Alexandrovna and Leonidze, as I see myself, as my substitute in a sort of warm-hearted proximity to them, as their protector. What can I say? Go to them and kiss both of them affectionately.

The main thing is this: for twenty-five years this story has lived and gone on, entire and indivisible, gripping, all made up of *one* sound, at times terrible and bitter, at times fantastic, divinely translucent, and this story is my life, and my secret, solitary struggle, and poor Zina and Lyona are the victims of my fate and of my whole character, and you and your closest friends E. A. and G. N.[1] are also the most intimate part of this story. And all of them together found themselves side by side, once more under your wonderful sky, united by the totality of the warmth and natural beauties of your country, as though it were an indivisible whole of an overwhelming, all-unifying gust of passion. What a rare and precious truth! How wonderful that it was destined to be repeated once more.

Ninochka, I merely wanted to thank you and I am sorry to have let myself be carried away. I should not have written about it all like that—it's not clear, it's nebulous and weak.

And yet, taken all in all, it is happiness as it should be—serious, profound, fathomless and sad, just because of its boundlessness and its magnitude, weary and flooded with tears.

I kiss you affectionately. . . .

Your

B.

To Nina Tabidze

4 October 1955

Dear Ninochka,

Thank you for writing to me at such a moment.[2] You are not mistaken in me, I deserve it: let us live, I shall always give you my moral support. It is for this that I have lived all this time, this is my purpose in life.

I always sensed this terrible truth. It determined my views, my attitude towards the time we live in and towards its chief representatives, and my future. Poor, poor Titian, who had to

[1] E. A. and G. N. Leonidze.
[2] On the confirmation of Titian Tabidze's execution, two months after his arrest.

suffer this martyrdom! My heart always told me that. I suspected it.

But courage, dear Nina! I want you to live. It's important to me that you should live. I need you in order to keep my senses, to bring our common answer to its conclusion, to endure all. I kiss you affectionately, my sweet one, my poor one, my dear one. . . .

Your
Borya

. . . Our travellers arrived safely. Everything at home is all right. Many, many thanks to you and the Leonidze family. E. A. often appears in Leonidze's photographs. She is beautiful! The most outstanding figure in all groups, bigger, more outstanding, more expressive than any of them.

Yes—a commission for you! I received an invitation from Abashidze and Chilaya to the Guramishvili celebrations. I do not know the address to which to telegraph my thanks and apologies for not going and not being able to go. Could you tell them that from me?

. . . Forgive me for writing so little to you. Give my regards also to the Chikovani family. There were very vivid, brilliant pages in his poem on Guramishvili.

1957

To Nina Tabidze

21 August 1957

Dear Nina,

I continue to be grieved and worried by the news about your bad health and physical sufferings. I understand it only too well, having gone through the same thing not so long ago.

In this letter I shall enclose a few poems I wrote towards the end of winter (before my illness) and four new ones I wrote after our removal from Uzkoye to the country. Just before I fell ill my last recollections were: the revision of *Maria Stuart* for the stage, two birthday parties in town and, generally, the appearance of the town on a winter evening on my arrival from the snow-covered fields. As always, I wanted to say it all in one poem. I imagined I saw something of what the ancients called bacchanalia,[1] an expression describing an orgy on the eve of some religious rite, a mixture of frivolity and mystery. And then I fell ill.

I knew that if after my recovery I resumed my work, which

[1] Pasternak's poem *Bacchanalia* was published by *Novy Mir* in the January number, 1965.

the hospital and convalescent home had interrupted, I mean, the writing and accumulation of poems for a new book, I should not be able to escape from this cluster of winter impressions and to move on further until I had paid my tribute to that idea of mine.

This is the origin of the winter poem in summertime.

Your

B. P.

To Nina Tabidze

30 August 1957

Dear Nina,

I am always forgetting to write to you about Titian's book. This is your great success. You can be proud of what you have done and achieved. I congratulate you with all my heart upon these fruits of your anxieties, exertions and efforts.

Generally speaking, it is difficult to talk of art or of poetry in this exceptional case, just as if one tried to analyse these subtleties on a scaffold. . . .

The translations of Tikhonov, Antokolsky, Zabolotsky, and everyone else without exception are very, very good. The translations of Seryozha Spassky are perhaps the best for their comprehensiveness and lyrical intensity. There is not a single one of my translations in which misprints did not obscure the meaning to a point of incomprehensibility. This is Starostin's[1] fault, for he did not take the trouble to send me the proofs in which I could have corrected these mistakes. But I don't suppose this is of any interest to you. I shall write about it to Bebutov and ask him not to repeat them in the Tiflis edition.

[1] A. V. Starostin, editor of the State Publishing House.

163

The best things belong to the last years, which make up the second part of the book. You are right: the presentiment of the end is present everywhere. I felt it in particular in the lines: 'Only he loves his hearth and his country who is threatened with their loss.'

Since everything depends on the quality of the translation and even the best translations cannot reproduce what constitutes the essence and charm of the original (it is impossible to divine it), one can only describe *The Meeting with Balmont* (translated by Derzhavin), *The Taparavansk Legend* (translated by Zabolotsky) and *The Birth of a Poem* (translated by Martynov) as happy accidents, which break away from the rest and produce an impression of dazzling freshness.

The chief motive power of Titian, the poet, stands out everywhere: the feeling of loyalty to life, to the history of his country, and to nature which, combined with the feeling of doom, adds a constant elegiac touch to the expression of his theme. There is a great deal of goodness and humanity in this, much more than in Paolo and myself, not to mention Esenin and Mayakovsky.

This quality of goodness in combination with lines of great imagery (as in *With the Mother's Mouth and the Infant's Lips, Like the Black Snow of Berlin's Streets, Where the Flock of Yellow Orioles Is Seen, But Those Are Not Orioles, But Mandarins*)—is the main and best thing in the book, its soul. . . .

I kiss you affectionately,
Boris

To S. I. Chikovani

6 October 1957

Dear Simon,

During my last illness I was separated for a long time from my usual way of life, its uninterrupted activity ceased for a time, nothing interested me, nothing stuck in my mind. It was, I believe, at that time that Zina or Nina brought me, at the hospital or convalescent home, the Russian translation (a very good one, of high literary quality) of your article on Titian Tabidze.[1] I put it away somewhere and forgot where.

I found it accidentally this evening during an unsuccessful search for the vanished typewritten copies of *Maria Stuart*. I came across the folded pages of your article and read it for the first time now.

It is a very good article, containing several striking, vividly narrated reminiscences, several important, serious, stimulating reflections, which are of more general significance and form a weighty, authoritative piece of evidence to which everyone will afterwards turn for information: the whole passage about the walk along Charchvadze Street, the whole passage dealing with the idea of *gadavardna*.[2]

I should like to say a few more words about your article. I find your remarks eminently correct when dealing with the question of the unimportance of the differences in poetry between simple, direct speech, unencumbered by similes, and those cases where it makes use of metaphors. Your examples

[1] Published as an introduction to the Tiflis and Leningrad editions of Tabidze's poems in Russian ('The Poet's Library').

[2] A reference to the following passage in the article: 'Titian Tabidze . . . possessed a sort of special disturbing intonation which he himself called *gadavardna*, which means "to throw oneself headlong, to take the plunge".'

from Pushkin and Baratashvili are very good. It is a mistake to think that these are elements of the written language or creative works. Actually, they were introduced into literature from colloquial speech which, even more than the language of artistic selection, consists equally of words used in a literal and in a figurative sense and in which, it seems to me, it becomes much clearer that direct statement and metaphor are not opposites but stages of a thought formed at different times, an early one, arising spontaneously and still unelucidated in a metaphor, and a quiescent one which has defined its meaning and is merely perfecting its expression in a non-metaphorical affirmation. Just as in nature many early and late varieties belonging to different periods exist side by side, so it would be senseless asceticism to limit the flow of mental life by the sole phenomena of merely the initial or merely the final order.

Lastly about intonation. In the past that word was applied to me in speeches and articles and it always used to arouse in me a feeling of unfailing dissatisfaction and bewilderment. This is too extrinsic and too poor a concept to contain anything fundamental and all-embracing on which to construct a theory even in the early days of social disintegration and street brawls.

I suspect that Titian used the term imprecisely and more than anyone else meant something different by it, something that exercised the power of a technical veto over me during the period of *My Sister, Life*, and if that was so, he was nearer the truth.

In 1917 and 1918 I was anxious to bring my poems as near as possible to extemporisation. The point is not that I tried to write the poems in *My Sister, Life* and *Themes and Variations* at one sitting or to alter them as little as possible, but that my reasons for doing so were of a more positive kind.

If before and after I used to concentrate on a poem till I believed it to be brilliant, profound, passionate, or powerful, in

1917 and 1918 I wrote down only what by the character of the language or by the turn of phrase seemed to escape me entirely of its own accord, involuntary and indivisible, unexpectedly beyond dispute.

The principle of selection (a very boring one, you must admit) had nothing to do with putting the finishing touches to the rough version of a poem or making it as perfect as possible, but simply with the force with which some of it burst forth red-hot and at a bound and owed its freshness and naturalness either to that fact or to chance and luck.

Forgive me for tiring you by an analysis of your own ideas. Here is the chief, tragic praise of you which has all the time been bitterly suggesting itself and which I refrained from giving, but shall all the same give to you. Your article is a token and measure of you yourself, of your losing yourself in such a welter of names and persons who came to a full stop somewhere long ago and far away and who can no longer be distinguished from one another. For whose benefit is the pulsing vein of your researches? For whose benefit is your elegance, the loftiness and compactness of your lonely scholarship?

Yours,

B. Pasternak

To Nina Tabidze

22 December 1957

Dear Nina,

I have long been wanting to ask Nita or someone else to let me know how you were, but every time something seems to turn up and I have to put off the natural expression of my concern. About a week ago Rodam brought to Peredelkino your letter written in pencil and almost illegible. I could make out some terrifying indications of your very high temperature. I could not help thinking that someone must have kept the letter a long time and that it was of an earlier date than the one we received by post.

I beg you to ask someone to write to me how you are feeling now.

Also, please, tell Simon, Konstantin Lordkipanidze and all of them that though I have not seen the *Literary Gazette of Georgia*, I received reports from everywhere about how nobly many of them had expressed their attitude towards me. Yevtushenko and Starostin told me about it, and Zdanevich and others wrote to me about it. I am terribly grateful to everybody for this. It makes me happy and keeps me going. . . .

I kiss you affectionately,

Your

B.

1958

To *G. V. Bebutov*

24 May 1958

Dear Garegin Vladimirovich,

My long stay in hospital is to blame for my failure to thank you till now for the book.[1] I could not help enjoying it. I do not like reminiscences, I do not like the past, especially my own. My future is immeasurably larger, I cannot help living by it. I cannot see any point in looking back.

You will ask why then I permitted its publication. I'm afraid I had to. New editions and translations are the material resources of my existence, they are bridges to the future, roads to the future, which I live for.

But my attitude to the book is one thing, and your introduction, your editorship, your care and selection, your research are quite another—you performed miracles in preserving and running to earth the different versions which I have so

---

[1] The last edition published during Pasternak's lifetime: *Poems About Georgia* and *Georgian Poets*, Tiflis, 1958. Editor and author of introduction —G. V. Bebutov.

completely forgotten that they do not seem to exist for me.[1]

Please, forgive me, for it is not for the first time that I have expressed my gratitude so insipidly and in so niggardly a fashion. It is not because I have grown ungrateful and callous. But more and more does fate carry me off nobody knows where and even I have only a faint idea where it is. It is most probable that only many years after my death will it become clear what were the reasons, the great, the overwhelmingly great reasons that lay at the foundation of the activity of my last years, the air it breathed and drew sustenance from, what it served. But to you—many, many thanks.

Your
B. Pasternak

To K. A. Lordkipanidze

22 June 1958

Dear Konstantin Alexandrovich,

I have long wanted to thank you for the attention and support which you have so generously given me during the last years. I received your telegram and in reply I can tell you that only *July* was published once in *Znamya*. The rest have not been published. I am enclosing a few more poems, written recently, after my last long stay in hospital. I am sending them to you just as a matter of interest, without any intention of pressing you to publish them, for I realise very well myself how boring and colourless they are. I am saying this without

[1] These texts were approved by Pasternak and are important as the last publications during his lifetime.

any false modesty and without any bitterness, for I cannot possibly produce any other poems now. I write them at odd moments, without real force and without sufficient inclination for many reasons. First, because as a result of my frequent, months-long, hospital intervals, time seems so in-between, so transitory, so unstable. . . . Secondly, even during the respite granted to me at the end of an illness and till I fall ill again (I never know how long that will last), the writing of poems means very little and cannot occupy a big place in my life. Besides, my correspondence with the West, which began recently, puts great demands upon me and gives me a great deal for different reasons: today about Rabindranath Tagore in answer to a question from his London biographer, tomorrow about *Faust* at the request of some museum at his (Faust's) birthplace near Stuttgart, and so on.

I press your hand warmly,

Yours,

B. Pasternak

To M. I. Zlatkin[1]

2 September 1958

Dear Mark Israelevich,

I am very sorry that, instead of being published with benefit to your publishing house, my book has made such a terrible loss. The receipts from 3,000 copies of the book scarcely cover half of what, according to the account I received in June, you owe me in lieu of royalties. Though I am forgotten to the

[1] Director of the publishing house Dawn of the East, which published a volume of Pasternak's poems and translations.

point of complete obscurity, I did not think I had been forgotten so completely that my book would not go through at least ten editions, which would have covered your expenses and the costs of publication. I realise, of course, that all this does not depend on you, for people in high office keep interfering with the future of literature; however, the rest are only too willing to follow them. Well, it's your business. It is a great pity.

B. Pasternak

1959

To L. Gudiashvili

3 March 1959

The weekdays during which one pays you a visit become holidays. On the day after visiting you one awakes with a feeling that everything one has seen and heard at your place has been a dream. A dream ought to be and to remain the only riches of the heart that cannot be compared with any other treasure—art.

To G. G. Margvelashvili

17 March 1959

Dear Georgy Georgievich,

... My wife and I were already in Tiflis when you wrote to me.[1] Of course, I shall be glad to do everything you want. ...

[1] Margvelashvili asked Pasternak to carry on with his translation of Tsereteli's poems. Illness prevented him from completing any new translations for the jubilee edition of Tsereteli's poems published in 1960.

We had a splendid time during the three weeks we spent at Nina Alexandrovna's, who put half of her house at our disposal and who showered love, care, comfort and repose upon us.[1]

I was glad to feel that indigenous and elusive quality in Georgian life without the traditional, excited elation, but all the more sincerely, sensibly and more verifiably, which hitherto I could not catch and express and which none of your artists have perhaps expressed (else it would not have gone on pursuing one in life, bringing one to a sudden stop and slipping through one's fingers). I shall one day set myself the task of getting to the bottom of it. It is something living, something that has been formed from the intermingling of contemporary urban life and nature and native types, but, above all, from centuries-old stratifications, two orders—festively victorious, threatening to turn into superficiality and later into something shatteringly tragic, doomed to silence, becoming more profound, fathomless.

I have spent a great deal of time in your museums and in what is a living museum or the continuation of the past in the present—among your artistic youth. I don't think I shall ever again experience anything more radiant in my life.

On my return home portents of dangers and sufferings awaited me. But everywhere in the world one has to pay for the right to live on one's own naked spiritual reserves. . . .

I thank you for remembering me and for your kindly attitude.

Yours,

B. Pasternak

[1] Pasternak's last visit to Tiflis took place in March 1959.

Biographical Notes

Afinogenov, Alexander Nikolaevich, playwright, author of *Fear*, 1931, which deals with the conversion to Communism of a Russian scientist. Another of his plays, *Distant Point*, 1935, deals with the people of a railway junction in Siberia and a Soviet corps commander, who is on the way to Moscow to consult specialists. He conducts a verbal duel about life and death with a former deacon in which the optimistic philosophy of Communism crosses swords with the 'rotten and poisonous' philosophy of individualism and pessimism. In his next play, *Mashenka*, 1940, Afinogenov deals with the younger generation in an attempt to show how the 'collective of Soviet people' help Mashenka to overcome the adversities of her life. His last play, *On the Eve*, 1941, deals with the war.

Akhmatova, Anna (1889–1966), poet. First poem published in 1907. Love lyrics 1912–15 established her popularity. After the revolution she published one book in 1923—*A.D. 1921*. After a gap of seventeen years she published another book in 1940. During her long period of silence as a poet, she published several studies of Pushkin. Zhdanov launched an attack on her in 1946, which led to her expulsion from the Union of Soviet Writers. She was rehabilitated a few years before her death and published some more volumes of poems. The themes of her poetry are concerned mostly with love and death and are treated with a tinge of mysticism reminiscent of the symbolist school of poets.

Annensky, Innokenty (1836–1909), symbolist poet who tried to introduce the impressionism of Verlaine and Mallarmé. Translated Euripides, Rimbaud and Baudelaire. Published a volume of lyric poems, *Quiet Songs*, in 1904 under the pseudonym of 'Nik-to' (Nobody). A second book of poems, *The Cypress Chest*, was published posthumously in 1910.

Antokolsky, Pavel (1896–), poet, literary critic and publicist. Member of Eugene Vakhtangov Actors Studio and later producer at the Vakhtangov Theatre. His first poems were published in 1922; he then published several cycles of poems in 1923 and 1928 dealing with Germany, Sweden and Paris, which he visited during the tour of the Vakhtangov Theatre in those countries. Since 1934 he has devoted himself exclusively to literature. Translated a number of French poets as well as poets of the different nationalities in the Soviet Union. In 1946 he was awarded the Stalin Prize for his poem *Son*.

Aseyev, Nikolai (1889–), poet. Began writing symbolist poetry in 1913. Published a volume of verse during the First World War and revolutionary poems during the civil war. One of the founders in 1923 of *Lef*, the left-wing literary journal. Greatly influenced by Mayakovsky.

Balmont, Konstantin (1867–1943), poet, leader of early symbolist movement in Russia. Between 1894 and 1906 he published eight volumes of poems, translated Shelley, Whitman, Poe and Calderón. He emigrated in 1918 and died in Paris.

Baratashvili, Nikolai (1817–45), outstanding Georgian lyrical poet, famous for his poem *My Steed* (*Merani*).

Bely, Andrey, pseudonym Bugayev (Boris) (1880–1934), poet and novelist. One of the chief representatives of Russian symbolism and one of its foremost theoreticians. Became a follower of Rudolf Steiner in 1912. His first writings appeared in 1902 under the title *Symphonies* (*Second* dramatic), followed by *First*, 1904, *Third*, 1905 and *Fourth* 'Symphonies'. His most famous prose work is his novel *Petersburg*. He is also author of works on the history of literature, and is recognised as a master of metre and rhythm, some of his work being written in rhythmic, musical prose.

Chikovani, Simon Ivanovich (1902–), Georgian poet. Awarded the Stalin Prize in 1947 for glorifying the benefits of the revolution in Georgia.

Esenin, Sergey (1895–1925), one of the great modern Russian lyric poets. Son of a peasant. Worked in Moscow as a proof-reader. Unsurpassable equally as a nature poet and as a poet of love lyrics, in which he depicted the eternally true and eternally different. Lived a rowdy café life with a group of Moscow poets, known as Imagists, whose theory was that the prime thing in poetry was imagery. Married Isadora Duncan in 1922, went abroad with her and after their separation returned to Russia in 1923. Suffered a mental breakdown in 1925, wrote a farewell poem in his own blood and hanged himself.

Fedin, Konstantin Alexandrovich (1892–), a prominent Russian novelist. A member of the Serapion Fraternity group of writers from its inception in 1921. The fraternity took its name from the hermit Serapion in one of Hoffmann's tales, in whose cave a variety of people gathered and told each other of their experiences. It played a great part, after a period of chaos and disorder, in bringing together older and more experienced writers and young writers demobilised after the civil war. Fedin published *The Orchard* in 1920 which was attacked by Soviet critics. His first novel, *Cities and Years*, 1924, was one of his earliest attempts to depict the effect of the revolution on the individual. His second novel, *Brothers*, 1928, deals with the mission of the artist whose right to individualism is opposed to the obligations of Soviet life. In the 1930's Fedin seems to have overcome his objection to the Soviet regime. *The Rape of Europe*, 1934–5, contrasts 'decadent' Western Europe with progressive Russia. His last works forms a vast trilogy depicting Soviet life from before the revolution to the end of the war. It includes *Early Joys*, 1945–6, *An Extraordinary Summer*, 1948, and *The Bonfire*, still being published as a serial in *Novy Mir*.

Leonidze, Georgy Nikolaevich (Gogla) (1899–1966), a Georgian poet. Studied at the Theological Seminary and at Tiflis University. His first poems were influenced by the symbolists but later he gave up his connection with the school and wrote in praise of the triumph of socialist construction in Georgia— *To Lenin*, 1936. He also wrote poems about the Georgian countryside and the history of Georgia. Awarded the Stalin Prize for his poem on Stalin in 1951. Awarded second Stalin Prize for poem in 1952.

Leonov, Leonid (1898–), one of the most talented modern Russian novelists. Born in Moscow but spent most of his childhood in the country. Joined the Red Army in 1920 and demobilised two years later. His first literary work consisted of poems showing the influence of the symbolist school. His first short stories are written in the ornamental prose popular at the time. The theme of the Russian intellectual is dealt with in his first novels, *Memoirs of Kovyakin*, 1913, and *The End of a Petty Man*, 1922. From the middle of 1920, Leonov gave up social themes in preference to themes of purely psychological significance. His novel, *Badgers*, 1924, showed a depth of psychological insight unusual for Soviet novels of that time. His next novel, *The Thief*, 1927, deals with the period of N.E.P. and shows the influence of Dostoevsky. It was followed by a short novel, *A Provincial Story*, and a cycle of country stories, 1927–8. His next novel, *Sot*, 1930, deals with the Five Year Plan. In spring, 1930, Leonov left for Turkestan and on his return wrote the short story, *Locusts*, describing the war on locusts in the district, 1929. His next novel, *Scutarevsky*, 1932–4, deals with the Five Year Plan, and *Road to the Ocean*, 1935, a semi-Utopian novel. His greatest novel, *The Russian Forest*, 1950–3, deals with the Second World War.

Between 1935 and the end of the forties, Leonov wrote a number of plays as well as some dramatic adaptations of his novels.

Mayakovsky, Vladimir (1893–1930), famous Soviet poet. Studied painting. Came under futurist influence and signed futurist manifesto in 1912. Joined Soviet regime in 1917. In 1918 he wrote *Mystery Buffo* and a verse play prophesying the victory of the revolution over capitalism, but his later plays, *The Bedbug*, 1928, and *The Bath House*, 1929, show signs of discontent with the growing philistinism and bureaucracy of Soviet life. In 1923 he joined Russian Association of Proletarian Writers. Committed suicide, 1930. In one of his autobiographical sketches Pasternak declares that he has never been on intimate terms with Mayakovsky. 'Mayakovsky,' Pasternak wrote, 'shot himself out of pride because he had condemned something in himself or around himself with which his self-respect could not be reconciled.'

Nadiradze, Kolau (Nikolai) (1894–), Georgian poet. Studied at Moscow University. First poem appeared in 1916 in the journal of Georgian symbolists, *Blue Horns*. His writings show a great deal of the influence of mysticism and nationalist romanticism. At first he was hostile to the Soviet regime in Russia, he later wrote on revolutionary themes.

Nadson, Semyon (1862–87), Russian poet. His poetry expressed the mood of desolation and despair of the Russian educated classes of the late seventies and eighties, following the utter failure of their attitude to build a bridge over the gulf that separated them from the peasants. His first poem was published when he was only fifteen. In 1882 his poems began to appear in various literary periodicals. His first volume of poems was published in 1885 and won him the Pushkin Prize of the Russian Academy. His poems are full of doubts and complaints against fate, of expressions of indignation at the sight of prevailing evil, of the consciousness of his own helplessness and of a feeling that the whole of his generation was doomed. They are highly rhetorical and struck his readers by their deep sincerity. A characteristic feature of all Nadson's poems is their clarity and logic.

Pasternak, Leonid (1862–1945), father of Boris Pasternak. Well-known painter and illustrator. After leaving Russia in 1921, he lived first in Germany and, from 1938, in England. Died in Oxford.

Pilnyak, Boris, pseudonym of Boris Vogau (1894–1937?), novelist. First works published in 1915. First novel, *The Naked Year*, 1922, deals with the civil war and shows life degenerating to an animal level. His *Tale of the Unextinguished Moon*, 1926, contains the hint that War Commissar Frunze was killed by the order of Stalin while undergoing an operation, which got him into trouble with the authorities. His novel, *Mahogany*, was refused publication in Russia and he had it published in Berlin in 1929. This led to his expulsion from the Union of Soviet Writers. In 1937 he disappeared and is believed to have been shot.

Pogodin, Nikolai (1900–), Soviet playwright. First play, *Tempo*, written round a Stalingrad tractor factory, notable for the fact that for the first time in a Soviet drama workers expressed very unflattering opinions about Communist commissars. His second play, *A Song about an Axe*, 1931, deals with the almost mystical powers of a metalworker who invents a marvellous alloy of stainless steel. His third play, *My Friend*, gives a realistic picture of a director of a Soviet motorcar factory.

Scriabin, Alexander (1872–1915), composer. Born in Moscow. Professor of the piano at Moscow Conservatoire. Pasternak first met him in 1903. 'Scriabin', he wrote in his memoirs, 'won me by the freshness of his spirit. I loved him to distraction.' Responsible for Pasternak's attempt to follow in his mother's footsteps by becoming a concert pianist. His most famous composition was his *Poem of Ecstasy*.

Solovyov, Vladimir (1853–1900), poet, critic and philosopher. His poetry gave expression to the symbolist belief that the world is a system of symbols, proving the existence of the abstract physical realities.

Tabidze, Titian (1895–1937), Georgian poet. One of the founders of the symbolist group of poets, 'The Company of the Blue Drinking Horns', 1910. Joined the Soviet regime after 1921 and wrote poetry glorifying the transformation of the Colchis marshes into citrus fruit plantations. In 1934 the 'Blue Horns' group was criticised at the Congress of Soviet Writers as 'fellow travellers'. In the purges of 1936–7 Tabidze was arrested and shot.

Tikhonov, Nikolai Semyonovich (1896–), Russian poet. His first poems were war poems written in 1916–17. He fought in the First World War and the civil war on the Red side. Greatly attracted by strong personalities, grandiose scenery and enterprises involving risk and danger. Next to Pasternak, one of the most successful translators of Georgian poetry.

Tsereteli, Akaki (1840–1915), Georgian patriotic poet. Known as the 'immortal nightingale of the Georgian people'. Many of his lyrics have been adopted as folk-ballads or popular drinking songs. In February 1907, he was arrested and imprisoned for publishing a lampoon making fun of the governor of Georgia, but was set free the next day because of unanimous outcry from all classes of society.

Tsvetaeva, Marina (1892–1941), poet. Began her literary work in 1910. Left Russia in 1922, but returned with her family in 1939. She was banished to the provinces where she could find no employment and hanged herself. Her poetry is distinguished by its exhilarating rhythm, fire and passion and its strong folk-song influence.

Vazha Pshavela (1861–1915), Georgian classical poet. Spent the greater part of his life in a small village in Georgian highlands. Author of epic and heroic poems depicting titanic powers locked in elemental struggle with supernatural forces and torn by profound psychological conflicts. Excelled as author of nature stories, many of which have become children's classics.

Yashvili, Paolo (1895–1937), Georgian poet. Went to Paris on the eve of the First World War. Returned home in 1916. One of the initiators of the 'Blue Horns' group of symbolist poets. He welcomed the establishment of Soviet power and wrote poems celebrating it, including a poem on the death of Lenin. In 1930's he wrote about the triumphs of socialist construction in Georgia. Translated Pushkin, Lermontov and Mayakovsky into Georgian. Horrified at the news of Tabidze's arrest and execution, and fearing a similar fate, he went to the headquarters of the Union of Georgian Writers, whose secretary he was, and blew out his brains with his own double-barrelled gun.

Yevtushenko, Yevgeny (1933–), Soviet poet. Entered the literary institute, 'A. M. Gorky', in 1951. First poem published in 1949. First volume of poems, *Pioneers of the Future*, published in 1952. In 1955 published a volume of lyrical poems under the title *Third Snow*. Another volume of poems, *Highroad Enthusiasts*, was published in 1956.

Zabolotsky, Nikolai (1903–), poet and translator. His early poems sounded like parodies of nonsense verse, but later he wrote in more orthodox style. Well known also as translator of Georgian poets. His first book of poems, *Columns*, was published in Leningrad in 1929.

Index

Index by Oliver Stallybrass